SCRIPTURAL HOLINESS FOR THE UNITED METHODIST CHRISTIAN

Mack B. Stokes

DISCIPLESHIP RESOURCES

MATERIALS FOR GROWTH IN CHRISTIAN FAITH AND LIFE

P.O. Box 189 • Nashville, TN 37202 • Phone (615) 340-7285

Dedicated to our two sons
Marion and Arch

Unless otherwise indicated, all scriptural quotations are taken from the Revised Standard Version of the Holy Bible.

Library of Congress Catalog Card Number: 87-72324

ISBN 0-88177-053-1

DR053B

CONTENTS

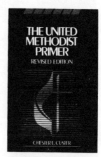

Also, read the companion book, *The United Methodist Primer*, by Chester E. Custer. (order no. DR024B) and *Beliefs of a United Methodist Christian* by Emerson S. Colaw (order no. DR025B), both available from Discipleship Resources.

INTRODUCTION

This book is about the greatest thing that can happen in the souls of people during their earthly pilgrimage. It is a book about God's call to holiness and the promise to supply it in ever-increasing abundance to all who truly seek God's purpose. It is a book about what the church and the whole world most need, namely, the sustained love of God and neighbor. At the same time, this is a book about the life-long struggle to move toward that "more excellent way" with God's ever-available help. It is a book about the biblical revelation on holiness and on the grace whereby alone we are enabled to begin and grow toward it. It is a book about Wesley's understanding of scriptural holiness and its pressing relevance for our time and place in history. It is a book about scriptural holiness for the United Methodist Christian and for all who earnestly and prayerfully seek the promised "more grace" (James 4:6-8).

The two words *scriptural holiness* steer us clear of the many pitfalls along the pathway of all who pray and strive for the highest levels of moral and spiritual living. The Old and New Testaments become the objective standard whereby we see the difference between the authentic and the inauthentic or the one-sided. Above all, Jesus Christ becomes our guide in our spiritual pilgrimage. For he is the author and perfecter of our faith (Heb. 12:2).

Our Risen Lord promised his own continuing presence to the very end of the way (Mt. 28:20). And, in addition, he called upon his followers to receive the "power from on high" whereby they could be equipped for the journey toward that holiness which issues in service (Luke 24:49; Acts 1:8). He showed us that this was no merely human venture. For it requires what he himself came to give through the power of the Holy Spirit. He taught also that this marvelous inner resource is made available not in isolation from others but in the fellowship of the people of prayer, faith, and service.

Under the power of the Living Christ, Paul carried out this quest in his life and teaching. He summarized it when he said, "For me to live is Christ" (Phil. 1:21). And he expressed what he had learned and felt from Christ in his inspired statement of what scriptural holiness is all about (1 Corinthians 13): It is not speaking "in the tongues of men and of angels"; it is not "prophetic powers," or understanding "all mysteries and all knowledge," or the "faith, so as to remove mountains." For without love these are "nothing." Here again this love is no merely human achievement. For it is the "amazing grace" of God at work in us through Jesus Christ.

Wesley took up this theme of scriptural holiness and gave it one of its most superb expressions in the history of Christianity in his sermons and writings on "Christian Perfection." He too recognized that the Holy Spirit acts directly and immediately within us, making for righteousness. For him, that direct and immediate action of the Spirit was seen and felt not in tongues, or signs and wonders, but in the miracle of the life pardoned and transformed by grace through faith in Jesus Christ.

For Wesley, the way to scriptural holiness was not in climbing the spiritual ladder to the mystical vision of God. Nor was it in the passion to be absorbed into the divine Being. Rather, it was seen in that "inward principle" which, by the grace of God, leads us directly toward deeds of love and mercy.

Wesley believed in the ethical life, in the earnest prayer and quest for justice, peace, and liberation. But scriptural holiness was something more than the struggling stream of duty. For it was the power of God at work in us as a clear and everflowing river of life—cleansing, refreshing, and moving us to do all the good we can. In summary, for Wesley, scriptural holiness was seen as "inward holiness" produced by the supernatural pardoning and re-creating power of God through Christ, which impels us into "outward holiness." The tree, being made good, bears good fruit. And, both along the way and in the end, the rewards are unbelievably great.

In his call to scriptural holiness Wesley was no sentimental dreamer. He knew the deepseated problems in human nature. And he was keenly aware of "Satan's devices." He could never have accepted the easygoing assumption that human nature is good, without recognizing the evil forces at work in us. For he was not oblivious to the biblical revelation. Nor was he blind to the problems generated by human nature itself. Therefore, Wesley was not naively supposing that God would simply supply the resources while we were passing and uncomplicated recipients. He observed carefully what holiness means in our thoughts, feelings (tempers), desires, and deeds. But this was done not primarily for self-analysis, but to point to the unutterable greatness of God's transforming and empowering grace.

The titles of many of Wesley's sermons remind us of his keen awareness of the need for the constant nurture of our souls in righteousness. For example, consider these titles: "On Sin in Believers," "The Means of Grace," the thirteen sermons "Upon our Lord's Sermon on the Mount," "The Nature of Enthusiasm," "A Caution against Bigotry," "Wandering Thoughts," "Satan's Devices," "The Cure of Evil-Speaking," "The Use of Money," "The Mystery of Iniquity," "On Schism," "Spiritual Idolatry," "The Danger of Riches," "On Redeeming the Time," "The Duty of Constant Communion," "Heaviness through Manifold Temptations," and so on.

Just as the body needs regular nourishment, so is it with our souls. And we need all the help we can get through prayer, mediation, Bible study, worship, fellowship, and service to others—always looking to Jesus Christ our Lord and Savior.

So we begin with scripture, moving through the Old and New Testaments, then to Wesley, until we turn inward, to our own yearning for that holiness to which the Master summons us. Finally, we move into the themes of holiness in our family life and in our responsible living for society and for the church.

CHAPTER ONE

HOLINESS IN THE OLD TESTAMENT

he Bible is our authority in all matters pertaining to Christian belief and practice. Therefore, we consider at the outset the biblical foundations for guidance on this subject of scriptural holiness.

In this process of reflecting on passages of the Bible, we should be aware constantly that God is speaking to us in the holy Word for a twofold purpose: first, to illuminate our understanding and, second, to call us to respond by faith and obedience. Every well-developed biblical teaching carries with it—in addition to something for reflection—God's call for our personal response. Therefore, a primary purpose for reviewing these relevant biblical passages is to hear the call of God which will move us into the life of scriptural holiness.

A large number of passages bearing on holiness might be selected from the Old Testament. It is a major theme. But I shall confine myself to relatively few. In fact you might wish to prepare or add your own selections. I have good reasons for lifting up the passages selected, and I will comment on them in sufficient detail for you to see their relevance and to hear God speaking through them.

God the Creator and Man in God's Image

In the beginning God created the heavens and the earth (Gen. 1:1).

Then God said, "Let us make man in our image, after our likeness; and let them have dominion over the fish of the sea, and over the birds of the air, and over cattle, and over all the earth, and over every creeping thing that creeps upon the earth."

So God created man in his own image, in the image of God he created him; male and female he created them (Gen. 1:26-27).

(The word *man* here has the generic meaning which includes men, women, and children. I hope this reminder will be sufficient to convey the thought that in none of my writing do I want to be sexist.)

Our understanding of holiness begins with God's unique ability to create. These passages which reflect on human origins and purpose are selected at the outset for two reasons. The first passage above fixes our minds on God who created us. The second calls attention to a starting point for understanding who we are and to Whom we are accountable.

Perhaps the greatest sentence ever uttered outside the Bible focuses on why God made us and is from St. Augustine: "You have made us for Yourself; and our souls are restless till they rest in You" (*Confessions*, I, Ch. 1). If God is our Creator, and if God made us for the purpose of opening our souls to the great heart of God, then this contains a divine summons. Do we hear it? The divine summons to what? To glorify and serve God forever. We can never be truly happy, or whole, or on our proper course, without lining ourselves up with God who made us for the glorious life which belongs to the children of God.

There may be other intelligent creatures on some distant planets out there in the unfathomable stretches of space. And God may have created them too in the same likeness or image. They too may be living souls made for God. But of these we know nothing now. It would not surprise me if such creatures did exist on many planets throughout so vast a universe.

God has not revealed either *how* he created the universe or *how* he created human beings. In one place in Genesis we read: "the Lord God formed man of dust from the ground, and breathed into his nostrils the breath of life; and man became a living being" (2:7). Does this tell us *how* God did it? Of course not.

Scriptural holiness is grounded in part on the conviction that all human beings were made by the Creator who is altogether righteous. And the Creator alone has the ultimate claim upon our lives. Without this, an essential link in the biblical teaching on holiness is missing. In this regard, the doctrine of God, the Creator, comes on the contemporary scene with renewed freshness and vigor. For in many lecture halls, laboratories, and writings today there are two assumptions which strike against this biblical teaching and, consequently, deafen people to the Creator's call to holiness. One of these assumptions is that the physical universe (Nature) is all there is. The other is that Nature is self-explanatory. Christians cannot accept either of these for two reasons. First, both assumptions run counter to the biblical revelation. Second, they drown the divine summons to holiness. There is an infinite distance between the way we feel about ourselves when we look upon a blind universe and say, "I came by accident from that?" and when we look up and say, "By whatever processes God chose, I came from the Holy Creator."

We know why God created us. And this ability to know why and to seek further understanding, is the quality that enables us to strive for a holy relationship with God. There is no need to talk to people of holiness unless they have a capacity for it. We do not say to birds, monkeys, dogs, and fish, "You must strive for holiness." Why? They have no capacity for it. We human beings are the only known creatures on earth of whom it can be said that they were created "in the image of God." What is this "image of God"? Among other things, it means that there is a special kinship between us and God. Put it this way: God is good; God is the Creator of beautiful things; God is the God of truth; and God is holy. Goodness, beauty, truth, and holiness—these are the ideal values. And these ideal values are neither new nor old but everlasting because they are ultimately grounded in God who is from everlasting to everlasting.

God created us with the capacity for growing and adventuring along these lines of virtue. We are sinners in need of God's help. Nevertheless, we are created to be bearers of God's grace. What if it were true that God made us for the purpose of weaving into the fabric of a passing earthly life those qualities which are neither new nor old but everlasting! What if it were true that we are so made that we can never be fulfilled, or whole, or happy, or redeemed unless we open our lives to the God of goodness, beauty, truth, and holiness! And what if it were true that we are made to join hands with our fellow human beings in this holy pilgrimage with God!

The "image of God" means that, among all known creatures, we alone were created to become the children of God and so to belong in the family of God. This means that by creation God has set his mark and seal upon us and claimed us for himself. On the basis of the first chapter of Genesis, and we might add Psalm 8, we see that this is a prime fact of our existence as human beings. It is this profound God-ordained reality about human beings which makes the spiritual disaster of human sin take on such awesome proportions in the Bible. More than any other prophet, Ezekiel saw the horror of repudiating God's call to holiness because he had such an exalted vision of the cosmic dimensions of the created order and glory of God's holiness.

Holy and Transcendent God

And the Lord said to Moses, "Say to all the congregation of the people of Israel, You shall be holy; for I the Lord your God am holy" (Lev. 19:1-2).

Consecrate yourselves therefore, and be holy; for I am the Lord your God (Lev. 20:7).

In the year that King Uzziah died I saw the Lord sitting upon a throne, high and lifted up; and his train filled the temple. And above him stood the seraphim; each had six wings: with two he covered his face, and with two he covered his feet, and with two he flew. And one called to another and said:

> 'Holy, holy, holy is the Lord of hosts;
> the whole earth is full of his glory'
> (Isa. 6:1-3; Cf. Ps. 99:5, 9).

> " . . . I am God and not men,
> the Holy One in your midst . . . "
> (Hosea 11:9).

Because God is holy and transcendent, God seeks and requires holy living. But what does it mean to speak of God as holy? In part, God is alone and transcendent in his greatness, perfection, and purity. God is so much greater than this imperfect world, and so much greater than this sinful suffering human race, that we cannot help feeling the sense of wonder, awe, and even the sense of dread in God's presence. For God is over and above and beyond the whole universe and beyond all realms of possible creation. Certain ancient Christian thinkers, including Origen (c. 185-254), speculated on what God might have been doing before creating this present universe. How many worlds has God created? And how many more are to come? Such questions lift up the greatness and glory of God before Whom we cannot help but fall prostrate in wonder and awe. For, though transcendent, God makes his presence felt in ways that lead us to join in repentance and silence (Job 42:1-6).

God is immanent (dynamically acting in and throughout the universe). But here we have in mind God's transcendence. For the Creator is unutterably greater than what he created. Are we to suppose that God's energies are completely used up in creating and maintaining the universe? If so, how could God be God? At this point we have moved far away from the earlier thought of our kinship with God to the thought that God is wholly different from us. For we are finite, dependent creatures. We do not *have* to be. God *has* to be.

Isaiah saw this in exile when he said,

> Have you not known? Have you not heard?
> The Lord is the everlasting God,
>   the Creator of the ends of the earth.
> He does not faint or grow weary,
>   his understanding is unsearchable (40:28).

In addition, this greatness and glory of God—this holiness—suggests that there are vast ranges of God's activity beyond the laws of nature, which God established, and beyond the whole realm of nature. Again and again in the Old Testament we are reminded of God's holy manifestation in the form of the demand that God alone is to be worshiped (Ex. 20:3, 5). "For the Lord your God is a devouring fire, a jealous God" (Deut. 4:24). It is out of God's holiness that his judgment and "wrath" against sin and disobedience come (Ps. 11:5; Isa. 1:14-17; Hos. 9:15; Amos 5:21-24). Ezekiel speaks of God's "jealousy" and "blazing wrath" (38:19). Through him God says that "all the (people) that are upon the face of the earth, shall quake at my presence" (38:20). And again, "So I will show my greatness and my holiness and make myself known in the eyes of many nations (38:23).

There is a fascinating yet bewildering mixture of words about God's holiness in the Old Testament. In addition to God's holy transcendence ("high and lifted up"), to God's "jealousy" and "wrath," God is fearsome, terrible, unapproachable (Ex. 19:21; 33:20), and incomprehensible (Ps. 139:6). For God's thoughts are not ours; neither

are our ways God's (Isa. 55:8-9). There is in the Old Testament a
mysterious mixture of God's nearness and distance. This keeps the
people of Israel alert. They are to hear the holy God's invitation:

> "Come now, let us reason together,
>   says the Lord:
> though your sins are like scarlet,
>   they shall be as white as snow" (Isa. 1:18).

At the same time, they are made aware that they cannot always find
God at will. Therefore, we read,

> "Seek the Lord while he may be found,
>   call upon him while he is near" (Isa. 55:6).

At times when we read of what seems to be God's wrath, ar-
bitrariness, and destructive acts, we can understand why the here-
tic, Marcion (died in A.D. 160), said that the Christian scriptures
should not include the Old Testament. For he said that in the Old
Testament God who created this evil world is cruel and unjust. He
cannot be the same God as the One whom Jesus revealed. A great
many churches throughout the Roman Empire agreed with Marcion.
But the church repudiated him and his position on this matter. Jesus
regarded the Old Testament (the only scriptures then available) as
authoritative. So did the Apostles. And, in addition, the Old Testament, in marvelous ways, spoke to the moral and spiritual needs of
Christians throughout the Empire.

We can see our way through these difficult passages on God's
holiness and wrath (including his destructive acts) by three thoughts.
First, God regarded the sin of Israel as a gross, thoughtless, and
defiant trampling on the sacred covenant-relationship which he made
with Israel. And God had to make known the seriousness with which
he took their stubbornness and betrayal. God wanted to penetrate
into the souls of people. And that was never easy. For they were
blinded by pride, misled by stubbornness, deceived by bad associates,
demoralized by lust, and enslaved by destructive habits. God wished
to shake Israel to the foundations. Second, we need to see that in the
Old Testament there is a developing revelation of God's holiness. This
development did not take place within the great heart and mind of
God, for God was always holy. Therefore, this development occurred
in the ongoing life within the people of Israel to which God reacted.

Third, God, in his infinite love and wisdom, chose to reveal himself through the medium of human beings. God—out of his boundless love—chose to go through the long, involved, and trusting process of speaking through people in the context of history. And this meant that, even among inspired writers, the human nature and situations would be required as the media for revealing God's holiness.

Morally Perfect God

On this theme, consider the following references:

> Ex. 20:1-17; Pss. 51:1,6, 10; 24:3-5; 139:23-24; Jer. 31:31, 33-34; Amos 5:21, 23-24; Micah 6:8; Isa. 40:28-31; Deut. 6:5; Job 13:15; Joel 2:28.

In these passages we see the developing revelation of God's holiness in the Old Testament. Therefore the words, "You shall be holy; for I the Lord your God am holy," contain the divine summons to righteousness and purity.

When God confronted Moses in Midian, Moses was aware of the awesomeness of being in the divine presence. The ground where he stood before that burning bush was holy ground. And in the presence of the holy God of Abraham, Isaac, and Jacob, "Moses hid his face, for he was afraid to look at God" (Ex. 3:1-6). Then later, after leading the enslaved people of Israel out of their bondage, Moses felt this same sense of awe on Mt. Sinai. But, in addition, God revealed himself in holy opposition to idolatry and immortality. God did this through the Ten Commandments (Ex. 20:1-17).

Here again we see that God had difficulty getting through to the people. For even after their solemn vow to be faithful to God (Ex. 19:8), and even after they had received the Ten Commandments, they hurled themselves wantonly into the idolatry of worshiping the golden calf. When Moses came down from the mountain and saw it, he threw down the tablet on which were written the Ten Command-ments and broke them. The people had "corrupted themselves" (Ex. 32:7). And Aaron might have included himself when he said that the people were "set on evil" (Ex. 32:22). But under the leadership of Moses the people repented and were renewed in their covenant-relationship with God. This included their commitment to obey God's

Ten Commandments with their emphasis on God's holy and moral requirements.

This understanding of God's holiness in terms of absolute purity in righteousness—God's *moral* perfection—became visible further through the Psalmists and prophets. The prayers of the Psalmists for a pure heart show that they knew God's holiness to be absolute.

Have mercy on me, O God,
   according to thy steadfast love;
   according to thy abundant mercy blot out my transgressions...
Behold, thou desirest truth in the inward being;
therefore teach me wisdom in my secret heart. . . .
Create in me a clean heart, O God,
   and put a new and right spirit within me (Ps. 51:1, 6, 10).

Wash me, and I shall be whiter than snow (Ps. 51:7).

Search me, O God, and know my heart!
   Try me and know my thoughts!
And see if there be any wicked way in me,
   and lead me in the way everlasting! (Ps. 139:23-24).

This is confirmed further when the Psalmist asks:

Who shall ascend the hill of the Lord?
   And who shall stand in his holy place?

And he answers:

He who has clean hands and a pure heart,
   Who does not lift up his soul to what is false,
   and does not swear deceitfully.
He will receive blessing from the Lord
(Ps. 24:3-5; cf. Ps. 15; Isa. 33:14*b*-16).

Jeremiah communicated further this divine concern for inward holiness in these words:

"Behold the days are coming, says the Lord, when I will make a new covenant with the house of Israel and the house of Judah. . . . I will put my law within them, and I will write it upon their hearts; and I will be their God, and they shall be my people . . . and I will remember their sin no more" (Jer. 31:31,33-34; cf. Joel 2:12-13).

Other prophets carried forward this marvelous concentration on God's holiness as consisting thoroughly in his *moral* perfection. In fact, God's holiness and justice are inseparable for the prophets. As Isaiah put it:

> But the Lord of hosts is exalted in justice,
> and the Holy God shows himself
> holy in righteousness (Isa. 5:16).

God loves justice and hates robbery and wrong. And he will punish those who do evil (Isa. 61:8).

It is this holy God who breaks through the hard crust of ceremonialism—through which people are deceived into thinking themselves to be righteous—and calls people to repentance and real righteousness. Amos gives the Word of God on this, saying:

> I hate, I despise your feasts,
> and I take no delight in your solemn assemblies. . . .
> Take away from me the noise of your songs;
> to the melody of your harps I will not listen.
> But let justice roll down like waters,
> and righteousness like an everflowing stream
> (Amos 5:21, 23-14).

Micah was speaking for this holy and just God when he said,

> He has showed you, O man, what is good;
> and what does the Lord require of you
> but to do justice, and to love kindness,
> and to walk humbly with your God? (Micah 6:8).

In the Book of Isaiah this holiness of God comes to utterance in the form of God's concern for the oppressed.

> The Spirit of the Lord God is upon me,
> because the Lord has anointed me
> to bring good tidings to the afflicted;
> he has sent me to bind up the brokenhearted,
> to proclaim liberty to the captives (Isa. 61:1).

The prophet Zechariah summarized well the spiritual nature of God's holiness. "Not by might, nor by power, but by my Spirit, says the Lord of hosts" (Zech. 4:6). The term *Lord of hosts* suggests physical or military prowess. So let it never be supposed that the holiness of God is weak and ineffective. It is the very nature of God's holiness to be dynamically at work in mercy and grace and in his marvelous redeeming love (Isa. 12:6; 29:19-20). The divine holiness is always teleological, that is, moving toward the realization of the kingdom of God on earth.

For God is the Holy One. God's name is holy (Ps. 103:1; Isa. 57:15; Ezek. 20:39; 39:7, and many other passages). To say that God's name is holy is the same as saying that God is holy. In some of the most sublime passages of the Old Testament God is referred to as "the Holy One." This wording is especially notable in the Book of Isaiah (Cf. 1:4; 5:19, 24; 30:12, 15; 43:15; 49:7; and others). And it is found in numerous other books of the Old Testament (2 Kings 19:22; Job 6:10; Ps. 71:22; 78:41; 89:18; Jer. 50:29; 51:5; Ez. 39:7). It is this mighty affirmation of the Holy One of Israel which, despite Israel's frequent repudiations, gives this divine summons to holiness its unalterable direction.

In Deuteronomy 6:5 we find what is perhaps the highest utterance in the old Testament on God's holy requirements. It is, of course, the great commandment: "And you shall love the Lord your God with all your heart, and with all your soul, and with all your might." Here holiness and the love of God come together. For one's whole being (all) is required to be devoted entirely to the Holy One. And with this we must place the words in Leviticus 19:18: "You shall love your neighbor as yourself: I am the Lord."

Out of all of this it follows as the dawn the night that the things and events pertaining to the holy God are also marked by holiness. The Law is holy. The ark of the covenant is holy. The Sabbath is holy. The rightful assemblies are holy. Other places on Mt. Zion are holy. Human relations, when seen in the light of God, are holy. Leviticus 19:2 becomes a mighty recurring theme in Israel: "You shall be holy; for I the Lord your God am holy." This is the holiness-code. It breaks forth in the liturgical literature (1 Chron. 16:10, 35; Ps. 33:21; 103:1-5). And it comes to expression in the affirmation that the people of Israel are a holy people (Deut. 7:6).

In addition, we see that God's promises—which came out of his holiness—are made to assure his children that what God expects of them will be possible because he is always with them to sustain them, re-create them, and empower them. Job felt this in and through all of his terrible sufferings. The Book of Job was written primarily to counteract the ancient theory that all people who suffer tragedies and disasters do so because of their sin or because of the sins of their forebears.

Job's "comforters" came to him to tell him to confess his sins, to return to the Lord, and to give up his sinful pride. But Job, not because of pride, but because he knew his heart was pure before the holy God, refused to yield to their accusations. And he boldly declared his faith in the Holy One, saying:

"Though he slay me, yet will I trust in him" (13:15, KJV).

In the Old Testament, God, because of his holiness, takes the initiative to give Israel the power to see life through and to live for his glory. For God gives power even to the faint, whether young or old. And he gives renewal and strength to those who run and walk through life (Isa. 40:28-31). In the Old Testament, in wonderful ways, the thoughts of God's transcendent holiness and his gracious nearness are held together in the being of the Holy One of Israel (cf. Hosea 11:9).

Beyond all this, in the Old Testament there is the promise of the superabounding grace yet to come. From Abraham, through Moses, through David, and through the Psalmists and prophets, the holy God of the Old Testament was preparing people for the coming of the Messiah. They declared in one way or another that the new era of the kingdom was coming. It was to mean the coming of the One who would save the people from their sins and inaugurate new possibilities for holy living. The Messiah's mission as Savior of the world would be carried forward through the outpouring of the Holy Spirit. As the prophet Joel put it:

"And it shall come to pass afterward,
    That I will pour out my spirit on all flesh;
Your sons and daughters shall prophesy,
    Your old men shall dream dreams,
    And your young men shall see visions" (2:28).

The Old Testament prepares the way for the New. The Old Testament teaches that holiness is not a merely human possibility. For it requires a turning and a total commitment to the "Holy One of

Israel," who created human beings in his image, who is greater and more glorious than we can imagine, and who sets a standard of absolute moral perfection in righteousness and justice.

One of the marks of the greatness and glory of the Old Testament is that its outstanding characters were always looking up to God, the Holy One, for help. They did not abandon their own abilities and resources. But, over and beyond these, they looked up to God for help. One of the best clues to assessing your spiritual level of holiness is to ask: Where am I looking for help? The ancient psalmist said,

> I lift up my eyes to the hills.
> From whence does my help come?
> My help comes from the Lord,
> Who made heaven and earth (121:1-2).

God alone is the ultimate source of holiness. So let us look to God for help.

CHAPTER TWO

HOLINESS IN THE NEW TESTAMENT

This location of holiness in God reaches fulfillment as it comes to focus in Jesus Christ and in the Holy Spirit.

Holiness and Jesus Christ

he Messiah whom the Scriptures foretold came to be the Savior of the world and the inaugurator of the new era of grace. "The law was given through Moses; grace and truth came through Jesus Christ" (John 1:17). This does not mean that the law was done away with by the coming of Jesus Christ. For as Jesus said about his own unique mission, "Think not that I have come to abolish the law and the prophets; I have come not to abolish them but to fulfill them" (Matt. 5:17).

No words are adequate to describe the influence of the life, death, and resurrection of Jesus upon his followers. In him there was not only the fulfillment of scripture. There was the One unparalleled in scripture—toward whom the scriptures could only point. He was not only the inaugurator of the new era of grace: He was the living embodiment of it. In and through his own person, as the incarnate Son of God, he defined the nature and motivating principle of the Father's kingdom and righteousness. He defined scriptural holiness by showing in his own life what it was.

Jesus Christ was known to be "the Holy One of God" (John 6:69; cf. Mark 1:24). He was not merely another prophet, or another Moses, who was greater than the prophets as the deliverer and establisher of the people of Israel. He was the Son of God, the "Lamb of God, who takes away the sin of the world!" (John 1:29, 36; 1 John 3:5). He was the way, the truth, and the life, the mediator through whom we come to the Father (John 14:6). In his humanity, Jesus, though tempted as we are, was without sinning (Heb. 4:15). In his life he was "without blemish or spot" (1 Pet. 1:19; 1 John 3:5). One of the clearest and best summaries of all this in the New Testament is found in 1 Peter 2:22-24:

> He committed no sin; no guile was found on his lips. When he was reviled, he did not revile in return; when he suffered, he did not threaten; but he trusted to him who judges justly. He himself bore our sins in his body on the tree, that we might die to sin and live to righteousness. By his wounds you have been healed.

Long before there was the canon of the New Testament, the early Christians regarded the remembered words of Jesus as authoritative. Those words were kept alive at first through the apostles and others, including Barnabas, Mark, and Luke. As Christian churches were formed in many parts of the Roman Empire, the memories of Jesus began to fade. It became a practical necessity to write down what was remembered about the life and teachings of Jesus. Out of this came the four Gospels. These, and most of the other writings of the New Testament, were in circulation among Christian churches by the end of the second century A.D. A new awareness of the meaning of holiness was made possible in succeeding generations through the written records of scripture.

The Lord's Prayer

In addition to the unutterable glory of his life, what did Jesus teach about holiness? He began with the Father as holy. He prayed to God saying, "Holy Father" (John 17:11). He taught his disciples to pray, "Our Father who art in heaven, hallowed be thy name" (Matt. 6:9). Here Jesus was building upon the Old Testament idea of God as "high and lifted up," as over and above everything in his creation, as transcendent. It is as though Jesus were reminding his disciples that it is no casual matter to pray to the Father. There is always a certain mysterious distance and awesomeness about coming into the presence of God. For God is the Holy One who is "in heaven" (Matt. 5:45, 48). At the same time, paradoxically, the very fact that Jesus asked his disciples to pray to God as Father suggests that God is near, approachable, eager to hear his children and to respond to their cries.

Notice also that Jesus urges his disciples to pray, saying, "Hallowed be thy name." We said in our account of holiness in the Old Testament that there are many references to the *name* of God as holy. In fact to speak of the *name* of God is to speak of God. So when Jesus told his disciples to pray, "Hallowed be thy name," he was reminding them unforgettably that the Father is holy. Therefore, all our prayers are to the Holy Father who seeks holiness in all his children. According to Jesus, then, God is the ultimate source of the call to holiness.

The Sermon on the Mount

Because of this profound awareness of the holiness of the Father, Jesus called his followers to holiness of life. In a true sense, the entire sermon on the Mount (Matthew 5, 6, 7) is his summons to the holy life. But, for our purpose here, several verses enable us to hear the Master's call.

Jesus said, "Blessed are the poor in spirit, for theirs is the kingdom of heaven" (Matt. 5:3). **Who are the poor in spirit?** The word *poor* suggests abject poverty, helplessness, powerlessness, loneliness, and utter dependence. Therefore, the "poor in spirit" are those, on the one hand, who feel the depths of their need, the heartrending tragedy of their sin, the terrible reality of their solitariness, and the fearful fact of their finitude and death. On the other hand, the "poor in spirit" are those who feel also the utter inability of the offerings of this world—useful as they may be up to a point—to satisfy their deepest needs. The "poor in spirit" are those who feel with Peter when he says to Jesus, "Lord, to whom shall we go? You have the words of eternal life" (John 6:68). The "poor in spirit" are those who feel their absolute dependence on their heavenly Father for forgiveness, for the new creation, for empowerment, for eternal life. This is the beginning of scriptural holiness, to be poor in spirit.

Consider the words of Jesus: "Blessed are the pure in heart, for they shall see God" (Matt. 5:8). **Who are the pure in heart?** Kierkegaard (1813-1855), the outstanding Danish interpreter of Christianity, said that purity of heart is "to will one thing." That is one important way of putting it. Kierkegaard apparently meant that purity of heart is the policy or decision to do not what we want but what God wants. What Jesus had in mind must have been inward purity, that inward cleanliness, in which the soul is purged of all bitterness, hatred, resentment, lust, pride, envy, covetousness, self-abnegation, and is devoted wholly to striving to live as our Maker and Father created us to live. In a word, the "pure in heart" are those who love God and their neighbors as themselves. And this love, being pure, is not mixed with guile. In addition, this love is dynamic, motivated for action for the glory of God and the blessing of people. This is scriptural holiness, to be pure in heart.

Again, consider the words of Jesus:

> "You have heard that it was said, 'You shall love your neighbor and hate your enemy.' But I say to you, Love your enemies and pray for those who persecute you, so that you may be (the children) of your Father who is in heaven; for he makes his sun rise on the evil and on the good, and sends rain on the just and on the unjust. . . . You, therefore, must be perfect, as your heavenly Father is perfect" (Matt. 5:43-45, 48).

The power, born in us of God, **to love our enemies and to pray for those who persecute us,** is an essential element of scriptural holiness. This does not mean that we want our enemies to have their way in the world. Surely there is nothing holy in wanting a Nero or a Hitler to have his way! That desire would turn Christian love into an agent of the powers and principalities of evil. What then does it mean to love our enemies? In what sense does God love them? God cares for their elemental needs and, above all else, God longs for them to come home. It means truly, sincerely, to desire God's best for our enemies; and above all, to desire their souls' salvation through Jesus Christ. This is scriptural holiness, to love our enemies.

Jesus said: "Seek first his (the Father's) kingdom and his righteousness, and all these things shall be yours as well" (Matt. 6:33). **What does it mean to seek first his kingdom and his righteousness?** It means to get our priorities straight. It means first things first. We are made for God and can never be truly happy, truly whole, truly victorious, truly saved and in possession of the gift of eternal life apart from the eager, willing, striving, joyful determination to walk and work with God. Therefore, whatever leads us to put anything above the call of God is idolatry. Inevitably, this seeking after idolatry turns us into lost souls, inauthentic forms of human existence.

Whatever separates us from the family of God—whether injustice, money, property, friends, athletics, education, entertainment spectacles, alcohol, drugs, gambling, lust, taking advantage of others, laziness, fads, or anything else—is idolatry. As Jesus said, "You cannot serve God and mammon" (Matt. 6:24). Mammon may be thought of as symbolizing not only money but anything which is placed above God and his kingdom. All worthy things, events, and relationships can be dedicated to God. But God alone comes first. Then follows our responsible stewardship of all with which we have been entrusted.

Jesus spoke of the priority of God's kingdom. In addition, he said that we are to seek God's righteousness. Again, this means inner purity, cleansing from inner defilement, and the motivating, dynamic love of God and of our fellow human beings. God's righteousness is no merely passive affection or inner flow of joy. It is teleological, that is, headed where God is moving and toward what God wants. This is scriptural holiness, to seek God's kingdom.

How is it possible to seek God's righteousness? In John's Gospel, Jesus says, "If you love me, you will keep my commandments" (14:15). He goes further and uses the allegory of the vine and the branches. He says, "As the branch cannot bear fruit by itself, unless it abides in the vine, neither can you, unless you abide in me" (John 15:4). He adds, "I am the vine, you are the branches. He who abides in me, and I in him, he it is that bears much fruit, for apart from me you can do nothing. If a man does not abide in me, he is cast forth as a branch and withers. . . . By this my Father is glorified, that you bear much fruit, and so prove to be my disciples" (John 15:5-6, 8).

Here Jesus tells his disciples that in their own human resources alone they cannot enter into the life of inner holiness which leads to fruit-bearing discipleship. The resources of God's supernatural action are necessary. More particularly, God's grace in Christ is necessary. For it is only as Christ lives in us and works through us that we can carry out the divine summons to holiness. As we shall see, Christ lives and abides in us only through the power of the Holy Spirit.

Holiness and the Holy Spirit

The two words, *Holy Spirit,* are used together only three times in the Old Testament (Ps. 51:11; Isa. 63:10, 11). In the New Testament they are used more than ninety times.

The Mission of Jesus Christ

Throughout the New Testament the work of the Holy Spirit is related to the mission of Jesus Christ as the savior of the world and the inaugurator of the new era of the righteousness of God. The Holy Spirit acted in the **conception** of Jesus (Matt. 1:18; Luke 1:35). John the Baptist said, "I baptize you with water; but he who is mightier than I is coming, the thong of whose sandals I am not worthy to untie; he will baptize you with the Holy Spirit and with fire" (Luke 3:16). The Holy Spirit descended on Jesus like a dove at his **baptism** (Matt. 3:16; Mark 1:10). And a voice from heaven said: "Thou art my beloved Son; with thee I am well pleased" (Mark 1:11).

The Spirit led Jesus into the wilderness to be tempted (Mark 1:12). It was in "the power of the Spirit" that Jesus returned to Galilee (Luke 4:14). And he felt the power of the Spirit as he **ministered to the poor,** the captives, the blind, and the oppressed (Luke 4:18-21). In Matthew, Mark, and Luke we find relatively little on the Holy Spirit. What we do find is important, but the focus of these Gospels had to be on the life, death, resurrection, and teachings of Jesus.

The most important teachings of Jesus on the Holy Spirit are found in John's Gospel. (See especially Chapters 14, 15, and 16.) There we see that the coming of the Holy Spirit in full power had to await the completion of Jesus' earthly mission and his resurrection. There too, Jesus made it clear that the Holy Spirit's unique mission is to reveal the things of Jesus Christ and to glorify him (John 16:14; 14:25-26). Therefore, it was Jesus himself who made it forever impossible to separate the work of the Holy Spirit from his own supreme mission as the savior of the world and as the One who summons all people to the life of holiness.

In view of his understanding of the depths of sin, the Risen Lord made it transparently clear that this dynamic surging life of holiness was made possible only by the "power from on high." The disciples were to wait in Jerusalem until they received this promised power (Luke 24:49). The Risen Lord said to them, "Before many days you shall be baptized with the Holy Spirit" (Acts 1:5). We see from the Gospels that **when we speak of scriptural holiness we are dealing with spiritual power.** Where can it be found? How can we receive it? Again, our Risen Lord said to his disciples: "But you shall receive power when the Holy Spirit has come upon you; and you shall

be my witnesses in Jerusalem and in all Judea and Samaria and to the
end of the earth" (Acts 1:8).

The Mission of Early Christians

At Pentecost this promise was fulfilled. There and then the Holy
Spirit illuminated the souls of those in that Upper Room to realize for
the first time, in any settled way, that Jesus Christ was indeed the savior
of the world and the Lord of life. Earlier, Peter had made his great
confession of faith (Matt. 16:16). But shortly thereafter he denied that
he knew Jesus or had anything to do with him. His confession was a
lip-service. Not so, after Pentecost (see Acts 2:36-42; 4:13, 18-22). In
addition to this marvelous illumination, at Pentecost they opened their
souls to the infilling of the Holy Spirit so that Christ was truly, personally, Savior and Lord. This relationship with Christ is vital to scriptural
holiness.

It was no accident that the Holy Spirit came upon and filled those in
that place. Who were "they" (Acts 2:1)? They were the apostles and
others who had been with Jesus. They had a lively and holy memory of
Jesus and of what he said and did. Some had been healed by him; some
had been moved by the simplicity and glory of his words; and all of
them were brokenhearted over his sufferings and crucifixion. Though
they did not understand the full meaning of his resurrection, they
witnessed his risen presence. And the apostles had heard Jesus explain
his life and mission as the fulfillment of the scriptures. No other group
anywhere in the world could have experienced Pentecost at that time.
For they and only they knew enough about Jesus Christ to experience
the power of the Holy Spirit. This too confirms the Christ-centered
mission of the Holy Spirit.

There were certain outward signs of this outpouring of the Spirit: the
rushing of a mighty wind, the tongues as of fire, and the speaking in
foreign languages ("other tongues") (Acts 2:1-4). But what really
happened in addition to these outer events? As we have seen, the
disciples and others were given to see and know that Jesus Christ was
the Savior of the world and the foundation of his church. In addition,
the Holy Spirit gave the apostles and others boldness and power to bear
witness to God's great salvation in Jesus Christ. (Read carefully the
remainder of Chapter 2 and note what Peter preached; see also Acts
4:31; 5:28-32, 40-42.) From the Book of Acts we come to see clearly

that the primary mission of the Holy Spirit is to re-create the souls of people—to save them—in such a way as to *empower them for mission and in mission.*

Always in the New Testament this empowerment for mission was preceded by that inner cleansing which comes from the re-creation after the image of Christ. The work of the Holy Spirit was always Christ-centered. Therefore, because Jesus was good, it was always ethical. Scriptural holiness is through and through ethical, marked by moral integrity and purity which comes from the presence of the living Christ in the souls of people. The Spirit did not act as raw power. Nor did the Spirit act arbitrarily. For the New Testament speaks of the supernatural action of the *Holy* Spirit. Many times there were "signs and wonders" (Acts 4:30; 5:12; 8:13). There were miracles of healing (Acts 3:6-9; 5:16) and deliverance (Acts 5:17-21; 12:5-7; 16:19-34). But always these were connected with empowerment for the work of carrying forward the redemptive life-subserving mission of Jesus Christ.

It was this Christ-centeredness which saved scriptural holiness from spiritualism, magic, and all sorts of weird expressions of the spirit. Some have connected the work of the Spirit in special ways with sex. Others have related it to communicating with the dead. Others have tied the work of the Spirit to specific predictions and dates of things to come which have no real bearing on the mission of Christ. Still others have connected the work of the Spirit with their hunches and impressions and even made it a substitute for common sense. But none of these can stand before the teaching of the New Testament. Indeed, even in the days of the apostles, there was Simon who thought this power could be bought with money (Acts 8:18-24), as though it were some kind of magical or psychical possession which could be passed on from one human being to another.

Paul and Holiness

Next to our blessed Lord, Paul teaches us more than anyone else on holiness. Paul experienced this same sense of the power of the Holy Spirit to transform all who believe in Jesus Christ. His understanding of this came directly from the Risen Lord's encounter with him on the road to Damascus. Much in the way of growth in grace and insight took place thereafter. But that encounter with Christ was foundational throughout his whole ministry. **Paul knew he was a "new creation."** He knew in experience that he was a changed man. He was no longer a Pharisee of the Pharisees who wanted to outdo his peers (Acts 26:5). There was a new love, a new motivation, a new power, a new victory over sin. There was a holiness of heart through Christ. There was a new inner witness. He was now walking by faith, not by sight (2 Cor. 5:7). He experienced "the glorious liberty of the children of God" (Rom. 8:21) and knew himself to be an heir of God headed for a great destiny (Rom. 8:17). So he was telling the Christians at Corinth what he knew in his life-transforming experience when he said, "Therefore, if any one is in Christ, he is a new creation" (2 Cor. 5:17).

Paul understood that the power of the Spirit is the presence of the living Christ in him (cf. 2 Cor. 3:17). All else was secondary or derivative. Therefore he could say to the Christians at Corinth, "For I decided to know nothing among you except Jesus Christ and him crucified" (1 Cor. 2:2; cf. Gal. 2:20). And to those same Corinthians—who prided themselves on receiving a variety of special gifts of the Spirit—Paul felt compelled to write: "No one can say, 'Jesus is Lord' except by the Holy Spirit" (1 Cor. 12:3). The unbelievers and even many of the Jews were saying, "Jesus be cursed" (1 Cor. 12:3). The words, "Jesus is Lord," constituted one of the earliest Christian confessions of faith. But, said Paul, it comes out of the hearts of Christians who have been transformed by the presence of the living Christ through the Holy Spirit. He wanted those Christians to understand what was the basis of this great salvation in Jesus Christ. So he called them to "earnestly desire the higher gifts," which come through Jesus Christ (1 Cor. 12:31) "whom God made our wisdom, our righteousness and sanctification and redemption" (1 Cor. 1:30). For the higher gifts of the Spirit are those which are available to all believers and which bear directly on our salvation in Christ and on our empowerment for living.

How can the things which pass away, or which have to be transcended, save us and empower us for mission? What about the "tongues of angels," or "prophetic powers," or "faith to remove mountains," or good deeds, or martyrdom, or knowledge (see 1 Cor. 13:1-3)? All of these will pass away or be transcended (1 Cor. 13:8-10). But faith, hope, and love abide; and "the greatest of these is love" (1 Cor. 13:13). If we have any of these special gifts without **the love of Christ,** we are clanging cymbals, or nothing, or gain nothing. Christ did not come to give us the things which pass away, but the life everlasting. For what counts in scriptural holiness is the new creation in Jesus Christ (Gal. 6:14-15).

Paul goes on to say, "Make love your aim, and earnestly desire the spiritual gifts, especially that you may prophesy" (1 Cor. 14:1). Here Paul explains what he means by "prophesy," namely, speaking to people "for their upbuilding and encouragement and consolation" (1 Cor. 14:3). The Corinthians are looking for manifestations of the Spirit. So Paul says to them that since they are eager for these, "strive to excel in building up the church" (1 Cor. 14:12). One of the surest manifestations of the Spirit is to **build up the church and so advance the cause of Jesus Christ.** This is an important characteristic of those who express scriptural holiness. Along with this, holiness necessarily leads to prayers of intercession. So Paul prays for the Thessalonians saying, "May the God of peace himself sanctify you wholly; and may your spirit and soul and body be kept sound and blameless at the coming of our Lord Jesus Christ" (1 Thess. 5:23).

We may summarize Paul's teaching and witness by saying that for him holiness meant at least five things: First, it meant "a new creation," the new birth. And this meant being forgiven by grace through faith and formed into the image of Christ (Rom. 1:17; 8:29). Therefore, it was no longer Paul who lived, but Christ who lived in him (Gal. 2:20). This was inner holiness, because Jesus Christ was pure and holy. Second, holiness meant the power to conquer sin, temptation, and circumstances (Rom. 5:20; 8:1-2, 35-39). Third, holiness was the love of Christ working in and through him (Rom. 12; 1 Cor. 13). Fourth, holiness was the constant spirit of thanksgiving to God (1 Thess. 5:16-18) and the sustained habit of thinking about whatever is gracious and worthy of praise (Phil. 4:8). Fifth, holiness was the yearning for the salvation and nurture of souls through the churches and the empowerment for mission (Rom. 1:16; 1 Cor. 4:20; 9:15-23).

Several other passages in the New Testament call attention to holiness. One of these was partly quoted by John Wesley from the Book of Hebrews. The entire verse reads: "Strive for peace with all men, and for the holiness without which no one will see the Lord" (Heb. 12:14).

CHAPTER THREE

WESLEY'S BASIS FOR EMPHASIZING HOLINESS

ne of the most important aims of John Wesley was to lead his followers to "reform the nation" and "to spread scriptural holiness over the land" (*The Large Minutes*, as reprinted in 1791—the year he died. See Question and Answer No. 3. *Works* (Z), VIII, 299). His lifelong passion was to persuade people to experience vital, personal, inward religion and to show the fruits of it. What was Wesley's basis for emphasizing holiness?

The Authority of Scripture

Wesley relied on the Bible. From the beginning of his ministry until the end of it, without any waivering, Wesley followed the Bible as the primary and final authority in matters of Christian belief and practice. To be sure, in discussing many matters—and in his numerous responses to issues raised in his day—he used the clear reasoning of his logical mind. And he made "earnest appeals to men of reason and religion." But when it came to doctrinal affirmation, his final appeal was to "the law and the testimony." In the "Preface" to his published sermons, which he left unchanged through many editions from 1746 to 1787, Wesley said, "Let me be *homo unius libri*" (a man of one book) (*Works*, Vol. 1, p. 105; see also his use of this term in his "A Plain Account of Christian Perfection," in *Works* (Z), XI, 373). This phrase was not used casually in passing or as a kind of rhetorical flourish. For that would not have been characteristic of Wesley. He did not originate the phrase, but he selected it and used it to give strong utterance to what he profoundly believed. His conviction that the Bible was the only final basis for Christian belief and practice was stated again and again throughout his life.

This appeal to authority did not mean that Wesley read no other books. He was a voracious reader of books. And he urged his preachers to "read the most useful books, and that regularly and constantly." He even went on to say, "steadily spend all morning in this employ, or, at least, five hours in four-and-twenty" (*Works* (Z), VIII, 315).

At the conclusion of his work entitled, "The Nature, Design, and General Rules of the United Societies" (1743), he said: "These are the general rules of our societies; all which we are taught to observe, even in his (God's) written word, the only rule, and the sufficient rule, both of our faith and practice" (*Works* (Z), VIII, 271; see also *The Book of Discipline*, 1984, Para. 68). Early in his career, Wesley wrote as follows in his evaluation of a Roman Catechism, "For as all faith is founded upon divine authority, so there is now no divine authority but the Scriptures" (*Works* (Z), X, 91; cf. X, 141).

In one of his plainest statements on the authority of the Bible, Wesley said, "My ground is the Bible. . . . I follow it in all things, both great and small" (*Journal,* June 5, 1766). Toward the end of his career (1786), in his "Thoughts upon Methodism" he restated this when he said, "What is their fundamental doctrine? That the Bible is the whole and sole rule of Christian faith and practice" (*Works* (Z), XIII, 258).

Tradition

Wesley was keenly aware that in spiritual matters there were various opinions as to the final authority. For example, he knew that the Roman Catholic Church held that scripture and tradition were co-equal authorities for Christians. He agreed with the Roman Catholics in regarding the Bible as authoritative, but he denied that some of their beliefs were based on the Bible. Among these were: transubstantiation (that the bread and wine are actually changed into the body and blood of Christ), the seven sacraments (instead of two), purgatory, indulgences, and so on (*Works* (Z), X, 90).

Wesley refused to accept Roman Catholic teaching that both tradition and the Bible were "to be received with equal veneration." By tradition the Roman Catholics had in mind the deliverances of the first seven ecumenical councils. When we use the term *tradition* today, it is not easy to discern what we mean by it. In addition, Wesley did not agree that the authority of the church was above that of scripture. The Roman Catholics had said, and still say, an infallible book requires an infallible interpreter. And ultimately that infallible interpreter was the church through the Pope. Wesley said, "As long as we have the Scripture, the Church is to be referred to the Scripture, and not the Scripture to the Church; and that, as the Scripture is the best expounder of itself, so the best way to know whether anything be of divine authority, is to apply ourselves to the Scripture" (*Works* (Z), X, 94).

Experience

Wesley knew also that in matters pertaining to holiness and the spiritual life, some have claimed that their special revelations, or visions, or special religious experiences were more authoritative than the Bible. For example, certain Quakers claimed their own "revelations" or special moments of illumination to be authoritative. But Wesley would not allow the Methodists to be moved in this direction. He was aware of the many persons in the past who had gathered around them groups who would be carried away with these special revelations. Therefore he held fast to the only sure guide, namely, the Bible which is God's holy Word. This was a special problem facing Wesley. For example, Wesley challenged an idea of Robert Barclay, a Quaker, who said that "revelations are not to be subjected to the examination of the Scriptures as to a touchstone." In response to this, Wesley wrote: "Here there is a difference" [between Quakerism and Christianity]. The Scriptures are the touchstone whereby Christians examine all, real or supposed, revelations. In all cases they appeal 'to the law and the testimony,' and try every spirit thereby" (*Letters*, II, 117).

Wesley did not deny that people might receive private visions or revelations. He simply urged that these must be tested by scripture. Otherwise, we could not know "which might be of God or of the devil" (*Letters*, I, 325). In his comment on 1 John 4:1, concerning testing the spirits to see whether they are of God, Wesley said, "We are to try all spirits by the written Word: to the law and to the testimony!' If any man speak not according to these, the spirit which actuates him is not of God" (*Explanatory Notes upon the New Testament*, p. 913). Elsewhere, Wesley said, "Do not hastily ascribe things to God. Do not easily suppose dreams, voices, impressions, visions, or revelations to be from God. They may be from Him. They may be from nature. They may be from the devil" (*Works* (Z), XI, 429).

Wesley was aware that nearly every breakdown of common sense and practical intelligence has claimed as its source some special revelation. For example, there were those people in his day, as there are today, who claimed a special revelation on the end of the world. As Wesley said, "In 1762, George Bell, and a few other persons, began to speak great words. In the latter end of the year, they foretold that the world would be at an end on the 28th of February [1763]" (*Works* (Z), VIII, 350). Wesley opposed them in this, both in public and in private. In his *Journal* for February 21, 1763, Wesley wrote:

> Observing the terror occasioned by that wonderful prophecy to spread far and wide, I endeavoured to draw some good there-from by strongly exorting the congregation at Wapping to 'seek the Lord while he may be found.' But at the same time I thought it incumbent upon me to declare (as indeed I have done from the hour I heard it) that it must be false, if the Bible be true.'

On Monday, the 28th of February, 1763, Wesley said that he told the people of Spitalfields of the "utter absurdity of the supposition that the world was to end that night." His opposition was based on scripture. For the Bible teaches that no one knows the time of the end (Mark 13:32; Acts 1:7).

Original Sin

Against this background we can be sure that Wesley's concern for holiness was deeply rooted in scripture. In fact, he thought of it as mandated by the Word of God. He insisted on using the term *Christian perfection* because it was grounded in scripture (*Works* (Z), XI, 450). Wesley understood holiness in relation to the whole sweep of God's grand plan of salvation in Jesus Christ. Human beings are created in the image of God, and have fallen because of Adam's sin.

Consequently, all people in their natural or unredeemed state are subject to God's displeasure and in need of God's redeeming grace in Jesus Christ. All who have reached the age of accountability are sinners because they have gone their own ways in opposition to God's holy purpose for them. God loves each one of them with a love that no words can adequately state. At the same time, since God is holy and "hates every false way," and hates sin in all its many forms, God will judge all people and require them to give an account of themselves. Following scripture, Wesley spoke of this as "the wrath to come." And it was no accident that he and others joined in saying: "There is one condition previously required in those who desire admission into these societies—a desire 'to flee from the wrath to come, to be saved from their sins.'" And he added, "But, wherever this is really fixed in the soul, it will be shown by its fruits" (*Works* (Z), VIII, 270).

One of Wesley's longest treaties, which has liberal extractions from other authors, was entitled, *The Doctrine of Original Sin According to Scripture, Reason, and Experience*. It consisted of nearly 200 pages. There Wesley spoke not only of the sins of ancient peoples but of those of his own time. In this essay Wesley was concerned with "the wrath of God." Are we to suppose that the God who created us for a noble purpose, the God who is absolutely pure and holy, is indifferent to our sinfulness? For Wesley, the entire issue of scriptural holiness was at stake in the doctrine of original sin—a doctrine which is taught by biblical writers. He puts it this way:

> I ask, then, First, Are you thoroughly pleased with yourself? Say you, Who is not? Nay, I say, Who is? Do you observe nothing in yourself which you dislike, which you cannot cordially approve of? Do you never think too well of yourself? Think yourself wiser, better, and stronger than you appear to be upon the proof? Is not this pride? And do you approve of pride? Were you never angry without a cause, or farther than the cause required? Are you not apt to be so? Do you approve of this? Do not you frequently resolve against it, and do not you break those resolutions again and again? Can you help breaking them? If so, why do you not? Are not you prone to 'unreasonable desires,' either of pleasure, praise, or money? Do you catch yourself desiring things not worth a desire, and other things more than they deserve? Are all your desires proportioned to the real intrinsic value of things? Do you not know and feel the contrary? Are not you continually liable to 'foolish and hurtful desires?' And do not you frequently relapse into them, knowing them to be such; knowing that they have before 'pierced you through with many sorrows?' Have you not often resolved against these desires, and

as often broken your resolutions? Can you help breaking them? Do so; help it, if you can; and if not, own your helplessness.

> . . . Do you *say* nothing which you afterwards wish you had not said? Do nothing which you wish you had not done? Do you never speak anything contrary to truth or love? Is that right? Let your own conscience determine. Do you never do anything contrary to justice or mercy? Is that well done? You know it is not. Why, then, do you not amend? . . . You resolve, and resolve, and do just as you did before (*Works* (Z), IX, 231).

Again, Wesley says,

> Universal misery is at once a consequence and a proof of this universal corruption. Men are unhappy, (how very few are the exceptions!) because they are unholy. . . . "Pain accompanies and follows sin." Why is the earth so full of complicated distress. Because it is full of complicated wickedness. Why are not you happy? Other circumstances may concur, but the main reason is, because you are not holy. It is impossible, in the nature of things, that wickedness can consist with happiness (Ibid., IX, 235; cf. His Sermon No. 45, "The New Birth," in *Works*, Vol. 2, p. 195).

Wesley points out that a major difference between other ancient authors and the biblical writers was this understanding of "original sin." The other ancient writers recognized that "no man was born without vices of one kind or another." But they did not understand the depths of sin. He puts it this way:

> They were wholly ignorant of the entire depravation of the whole human nature, of every man born into the world, in every faculty of his soul, not so much by those particular vices which reign in particular persons as by the general flood of atheism and idolatry, of pride, self-will, and love of the world. This, therefore, is the first, grand, distinguishing point between heathenism and Christianity (*Works*, Vol. 2, p. 183).

Wesley goes so far as to say that "all who deny this—call it 'original sin' or by any other title—are but heathens still in the fundamental point which differences heathenism from Christianity" *(loc. cit.)*. For it is precisely this which makes the salvation provided in Jesus Christ *a necessity for all human beings*. Wesley is dealing here with "the mystery of iniquity" which runs as a primary negative theme throughout the Bible (cf. 2 Thess. 2:7). Wesley found it exceedingly difficult to get across to many of the educated people of his day the reality and awesome dimensions of sin. Therefore, in his sermon on "Original Sin," he says, "what must we do with our Bibles? . . . These accounts, however pleasing to flesh and blood, are utterly irreconcilable with the scriptural" (*Works,* vol. 2, p. 173).

Wesley believed that this divine revelation on human sin is a necessary theme because, if we overlook it, we will remain blind to our need to be delivered from the "wrath of God."* Wesley knew that we can face the awesome reality of sin in all of its life-destroying consequences because God has provided the absolute answer to it in Jesus Christ. Otherwise, it would have been too painful to reflect on it as Wesley did. Not only *can* we do this, we *must* do it.

Having made clear, on the basis of scripture, the depths of sin and need within all human beings, Wesley then went on to speak of God's gracious action in response to this fatal disease within human nature. He called this "God's method of healing a soul which is *thus diseased.*" For the great Physician alone can apply the medicine to heal this disease (*Works,* Vol. 2, p. 184). It is truly marvelous indeed that, as the Bible teaches, the vast resources of God's grace have been available to people so that they can be transformed and walk in that newness of life which moves toward holiness. Wesley wanted his followers to understand with absolute clarity what the Bible teaches, that apart

---

*Wesley made it clear again and again that in the Bible God has revealed the only way to "flee from the wrath to come and be saved from our sins." Parenthetically, we may say that by the "wrath of God," on the basis of scripture, Wesley understood two things. First, he meant that we are creatures with whom God is profoundly displeased here and now. Consequently, we are without God and without hope in the world (Eph. 2:12). Second, he meant that we are subject to the punishment which was yet to come for wrong living (cf. Mt. 25:31-46; Wesley, *Works* (Z), IX, 419). In and through all of this Wesley knew that even God's "wrath" is an expression of divine love. For what kind of God would love people and be unconcerned about their wickedness leading to their destruction both on earth and in the life to come? Wesley regarded this revelation on our sinfulness as of utmost significance in bringing to life those who are "dead through their trespasses and sins" (Eph. 2:1). Therefore, he wrote of "the unspeakable importance of thoroughly understanding this great foundation of all revealed religion" (*Works* (Z), IX, 434).

from the supernatural action of God—that is, apart from God's grace—there is no answer to our deepseated moral and spiritual needs. Only the divine medicine will suffice.

For example, in opposing the idea that we are the children of God "by gaining habits of virtue," he says:

> Nay, but, according to the whole tenor of Scripture, the being born again does really signify the being inwardly changed by the almighty operation of the Spirit of God; changed from sin to holiness; renewed in the image of Him that created us. And why must we be so changed? Because "without holiness no man shall see the Lord;" and because, without this change, all our endeavors after holiness are ineffectual. God hath indeed "endowed us with understanding, and given us abundant means:" But our understanding is as insufficient for that end, as are the outward means, if not attended with inward power (*Works* (Z), IX, 308).

Wesley's convictions about the call to holiness are based on the Bible. Those passages of scripture referred to in the first two chapters of this book figure significantly in his thinking. God is holy. Therefore, we are to be holy. "You shall be holy; for I the Lord your God am holy" (Lev. 19:2; cf. 1 Pet. 1:16). The various references in the Bible to the theme of Christian perfection, or holiness, or sanctification, are to be found in his essay, "A Plain Account of Christian Perfection" (1777; *Works* (Z), XI, 388-91). Wesley understood these to contain in them not only the call to holiness but also God's promise to enable us to receive it.

On the basis of scripture, we are to hear God's call to holiness and, at the same time, to be confident that what God has called us to, he is able to provide through Jesus Christ (Sermon: "The Scripture Way of Salvation," III, *Works,* Vol. 2, pp. 167-68). Otherwise, the call would be a mockery. But with God's call and the promised sufficiency of divine grace, we have one of the grandest of all the practical teachings of the Bible. This "inward holiness" which leads to "outward holiness" was no merely *human* possibility. As Wesley says, "We know indeed that 'to man'—to the natural man—'this is impossible.' But we know also that as 'no work is impossible with God,' 'so all things are possible to him that believeth'" (*Works,* Vol. 11, p. 67).

We are to ask, seek, and knock until we receive this holiness which God wants us to have (Matt. 7:7-8).

CHAPTER FOUR

WESLEY'S
UNDERSTANDING OF
HOLINESS

 **hat is Wesley's understanding of holiness? What is the scriptural way of moving toward holiness?**
Wesley frequently wrote on this subject under the term *Christian perfection*. Because the word *perfection* often led to opposition and misunderstanding, he went to great lengths again and again to explain what he did not mean and what he did mean. After all, do we not ask: Who can be perfect in this life? Is not that beyond us even by the grace of God? Are not our limitations of mind and energy so evident as to preclude perfection? Is it not vain to claim Christian perfection? Is it not another way of talking about works-righteousness? Wesley dealt with all of these and other questions. But he insisted on using the term because he said it was scriptural (see *Works*, Vol. 2, pp. 99-100).

How Christians Are Not Perfect

Wesley's tract entitled "A Plain Account of Christian Perfection" underwent revisions and enlargements during his lifetime, until the year 1777. In this, as well as in his two sermons entitled "Christian Perfection" and "On Perfection," Wesley tells in detail what he does not mean by "Christian perfection" or holiness (*Works* (Z), XI, 366-446; see also *Works*, Vol. 2, pp. 99-124; Vol. 3, pp. 71-87). Wesley says that Christian perfection is "only another name for holiness" (*Works*, Vol. 2, p. 104; cf. *Works* (Z), XI, pp. 450-51).

In his sermon entitled "Christian Perfection," he shows in what sense Christians are **not perfect.** "They are not perfect **in knowl-**

edge: they are not so perfect in this life as to be free from ignorance. They know many things in common with others which involve a working relationship with this world. And they know what is necessary for their salvation—the things which are "spiritually discerned." They know God's love—"the mighty working of His Spirit" in their hearts. They know what God requires of them and how to keep a clear conscience before God and toward others.

But beyond these, there are innumerable things about Almighty God which Christians do not know. They do not understand the Trinity, the Incarnation, the times and seasons of God's action, or why things may happen to them as they do. They do not understand the unfathomable dimensions of the universe and the actions of the Almighty in creating and sustaining it. "So great is the ignorance, so very little the knowledge of even the best of men" (See on this, *Works,* Vol. 2, pp. 100-101).

Again, Wesley says that no one is so perfect in this life as to be free from **mistakes.** These are consequences of our ignorance. As Wesley states:

> 'Tis true the children of God do not mistake as to the things essential to salvation. They do not 'put darkness for light, light for darkness,' neither 'seek death in the error of their life.' For they are 'taught of God,' and the way which he teaches them, the way of holiness, is so plain that 'the wayfaring man, though a fool, need not err therein.' But in things unessential to salvation they do err, and that frequently. The best and wisest of men are frequently mistaken even with regard to facts; believing those things not to have been which really were, or those to have been done which were not (*Works,* Vol. 2, p. 102).

For this reason they may misjudge others. And even in regard to the Bible, "the best of men are liable to mistakes," particularly in reference to those passages which "less immediately relate to practice." Why otherwise would the apostles write to the Christians saying, "Let no one deceive you"? (Eph. 5:6; 1 John 3:7).

Moreover, the true Christian is not free from **infirmities.** By infirmities here Wesley does not mean those things often referred to such as drunkenness, uncleanness, taking God's name in vain, or saying of another person "thou fool," or returning "railing for railing." Of these Wesley says, "It is plain that all who thus speak, if ye repent not, shall with your infirmities go quick to hell" (*Works*, Vol. 2, p. 103). What he has in mind by infirmities which true Christians may have are: inward and outward weakness such as slowness of understanding, confusedness of apprehension, incoherence of thought, "irregular quickness or heaviness of imagination," and the lack of a retentive memory. From these follow such other imperfections as "slowness of speech, impropriety of language, ungracefulness of pronunciation—to which one might add a thousand nameless defects either in conversation or behavior." "These," says Wesley, "are the infirmities which are found in the best of men in a larger or smaller proportion. And from these none can hope to be perfectly freed till the spirit returns to God that gave it" (*Works*, Vol. 2, p. 103).

In addition, Wesley says that we cannot expect to be wholly free from **temptation** (*Works*, Vol. 2, p. 104; Vol. 11, p. 339). And Christian perfection, or holiness, is not a fixed state beyond which we are not required to grow and to act. It is not a release from doing good, from attending public worship, and from cultivating the spiritual life through prayer, meditation, and returning to the Word of God. As Wesley puts it, "There is no 'perfection of degrees,' as it is termed; none which does not admit of a continual increase. So that how much soever any man hath attained, or in how high a degree soever he is perfect, he hath still need to 'grow in grace,' and daily to advance in the knowledge and love of God his Saviour" (*Works*, Vol. 2, pp. 104-105). And it is not a fixed state from which none can backslide.

In his sermon entitled, "On Perfection," Wesley takes a somewhat different turn and says that he does not mean the perfection of angels. Nor does he mean Adam's perfection—the perfection of Adam before his disobedience. Then he goes on to speak of "ignorance and error, and a thousand other infirmities" (*Works*, Vol. 3, pp. 72-73).

From other things that Wesley said, we can see that he did **not** mean to identify scriptural holiness with any of the **special gifts** of the Holy Spirit such as those on which Paul gave wise counsel (see 1 Cor. 12:4-11; 14:1-5, 9-12, 26; Eph. 4:11-12). Scriptural holiness is not for a select few but for all who open their souls with others to the infilling of the Holy Spirit. Wesley joined Paul in calling people to "the more excellent way" (1 Cor. 12:31; and chapter 13; see Wesley's sermon entitled "The More Excellent Way" in *Works*, Vol. 3, pp. 263-77). In his sermon of that title, Wesley says that this more excellent way is "far more desirable than all these [special gifts] put together, inasmuch as it will infallibly lead you to happiness both in this world and in the world to come; whereas you might have all those gifts, yea, in the highest degree, and yet be miserable both in time and eternity" (*Works*, Vol. 3, p. 263; 1 Cor. 13:1-3). Again and again Wesley **denied** that he had any extraordinary measure of the Spirit (*Works*, Vol. 11, p. 468).

Some people have identified holiness with an emotional experience of joy in the Lord. But Wesley's teaching was **not based on emotional joy.** For example, when one of his rather gifted preachers wrote him that "holiness consisted in a flow of joy," Wesley wrote: "I constantly told you quite the contrary: I told you it was love; the love of God and our neighbor; the image of God stamped on the heart; the life of God in the soul of man; the mind that was in Christ, enabling us to walk as Christ also walked" (*Journal*, V, 283-84). It is very easy for us to shout, "Glory!" "Praise God!" "Hallelujah!" All of us feel at times—or are entitled to it—a sense of profound joy or peace because of all that God has done and is doing for us and in us. And there is something essentially right about singing the doxologies together, for all blessings flow from God. But Wesley was not willing to let this be more than an accompanying factor attending scriptural holiness.

Once more, Wesley said that scriptural holiness was **not to be identified with mystical visions or mystical union with God.** He started out with much appreciation of William Law. But as early as 1738 he broke with Law because he had moved away into the realms of mystical ecstasy. Very early in his ministry Wesley saw that if he had followed the teaching of Jakob Boehme (1575-1624), a German mystic generally known in England as Jacob Behmen, he would have had to give up the Bible. For Boehme said that "God was never angry at sinners." To which Wesley responded: "But, if so, he was never reconciled to them. His wrath was never turned away, if it never existed. And, admitting this, there is no place for justification; nor, consequently, for faith in a pardoning God, which is the root of both inward and outward holiness" (*Works* (Z), IX, p. 513).

He thought of another mystic, Madame Guyon (1648-1717), as a good woman who wrote well, but whose teachings led to "unscriptural quietism." Wesley felt that the mystics, especially Boehme and William Law, tended to be very obscure in their writings. But, far more than this, they struck against God's revealed ways of leading people into inward and outward holiness (See *Works* (Z), IX, pp. 466-518). In addition, Boehme's teaching in particular "strikes at the root of external religion, by destroying zeal for good works; by laying little stress on either works of piety or mercy, and still less upon Christian society" (*Works* (Z), IX, pp. 513-14).

Holiness Is the Love of God and Neighbor

What then did Wesley mean by scriptural holiness? He had several ways of expressing it, but they all came to the same thing. As Wesley said, "It is all comprised in that one word, *love*" (*Works*, Vol 3, p. 74). It is the love of God and neighbor. More particularly, scriptural holiness is, as the Bible teaches, first loving God with all our heart, soul, mind, and strength; and second, loving our neighbor as ourselves (Mark 12:30-31; Matt 22:37-39; Luke 10:27; Deut. 6:5; Lev. 19:18). Wesley referred to the first of these two great commandments as the "royal law of heaven and earth" (*Works* (Z), IX, p. 368). Characteristically, again and again Wesley would call attention to what it means to love God with *all* our heart, soul, mind, and strength, and to love our neighbor *as ourselves.*

In all of this—on the basis of scripture—Wesley combined the dimension of faith with the ethical dimension. For these two were always joined together in the great heart of God. And human beings were not to put asunder what God had joined together. It is love alone that "binds everything together in perfect harmony" (Col. 3:14). Wesley's writings on holiness, or Christian perfection, represent one of the greatest efforts in the history of Christianity to reform, moralize, and transform human beings, His primary concern is to proclaim God's call to press on toward that holiness and excellence promised by God and available by grace. Albert C. Outler speaks of this as the "farthest reach of grace" (*Works*, Vol. 2, p. 97).

Another way of expressing scriptural holiness was in terms of the "new nature, created after the likeness of God in true righteousness and holiness" (Eph. 4:24; Col. 3:10). It is that change wrought in the soul by grace so that it is recreated after the image of Christ (cf. Rom. 8:29; Eph. 2:10).

Wesley said that the image of Christ is to have "the whole disposition of his [Christ's] mind, all his affections, all his tempers, both toward God and man" (*Works*, Vol. 3, p. 74). This means that, by the mighty action of God in us, we are motivated by the inner presence of Christ with the desire and will to love God and neighbor and to walk as Jesus walked. It means "an entire inward and outward conformity to our Master" (*Works* (Z), XI, p. 367). "It is that habitual disposition of the soul which, in the sacred writings, is termed holiness" (*Works* (Z), XI, p. 367). "The essence of Christian holiness is simplicity and purity; one design, one desire—entire devotion of God" (*Letters*, V, p. 238).

The Victory and the Fruit

Two other images are needed to give a more fully delineated picture of Wesley's understanding of scriptural holiness. The first has to do with the victory over sin; the second, with the fruit of holiness. Wesley made much of the power of the Holy Spirit to enable us to gain the victory over temptation and sin. This was no casual passing thought. He devoted over half of his sermons on "Christian Perfection," to showing that mature Christians, "all real Christians," are free from sin (*Works*, Vol. 2, pp. 105-21). That is, as long as they are holding fast to the Savior, and are transformed by the Holy Spirit, it is not their nature to sin. Wesley defines sin as "a voluntary transgression of a known law" (*Works* (Z), XI, p. 396; XII, p. 394). For example, Wesley asks, "Where do evil thoughts come from?" Out of the heart. "If therefore the heart be no longer evil, then evil thoughts can no longer proceed out of it. If the tree were corrupt, so would be the fruit. But the tree is good. The fruit therefore is good also" (*Works*, Vol. 2, p. 117). So is it with the whole range of life, from "evil tempers," evil words, and evil deeds of all kinds.

Does not this leave room for pride and self-righteousness? Not as Wesley presents it. For only by the transforming supernatural action of the grace of God is holiness made possible. Love for God and the consequent love of our fellow human beings, even our enemies—that is the essence of scriptural holiness. And, according to Wesley, this direct action of the Holy Spirit is seen primarily, not in any of the special gifts of the Spirit, but in the dynamic presence of the Holy Spirit filling our souls with that inward love which manifests itself in outward deeds. Wesley thought of this infilling with love as definite, immediate, and dynamic here and now.

The Scriptural Way to Holiness

The way is by grace through faith (Eph. 2:8). This was one of Wesley's favorite texts. From 1738 until his death in 1791, there are around sixty instances of his using it in his preaching. Everything in the Christian life comes from the grace of God in Christ. And this grace is the power of the Holy Spirit.

When we first think of it, we cannot but be struck by Wesley's strong emphasis on original sin, on the one hand, and his passionate concern for holiness on the other. How can human beings, who are so devoid of good, ever be holy? And, more than that, why not join the cynics of all ages and leave these fallen creatures to continue to sink like stones to the bottom of the sea? Why not let it go at that?

This was an impossible option for Wesley. Why? Because he believed in the marvelous salvation through Jesus Christ which is revealed in the Bible. It was precisely in the light of the desperate plight of human beings that Wesley saw the glory and supernatural power of God in Christ. Therefore, we must fix in our minds firmly that, for Wesley, scriptural holiness is no human achievement. For it is possible only by the grace of God in Christ made available through the power of the Holy Spirit. It comes by faith alone. It is precisely in the light of human weakness and sinfulness, and in the light of the failure of anything this world has to offer, that Wesley sees the glory of the "amazing grace" of God.

Both justification (God's pardoning grace) and sanctification (God's highest level of grace) are available only by faith. That is, the only condition of our receiving these is faith, which the Holy Spirit awakens in us. Repentance is only "remotely necessary," because we can repent from now until doomsday and still not be pardoned for our sins. The same is true of good deeds which we must do if we are to continue to be saved. For good works depend upon time and opportunity. But faith is *"immediately* and *proximately* necessary"* both for justification and sanctification (see the sermon on "The Scripture Way of Salvation," *Works,* Vol. 2, pp. 163-67).

In Wesley's emphasis on the grace of God relative to our sinfulness and weakness, he was following the path which Paul trod before him (see especially Rom. 5:20-21; 2 Cor. 12:9). For it is in the midst of our weakness and inadequacy that we know the "power of Christ" which is "the power of God for salvation to every one who has faith" (Rom. 1:16).

No words are adequate to express how strongly Wesley believed in the power of God's grace to pardon our sins, to recreate our souls after the image of Christ, to enable us to gain the victory over temptation and sin, and to follow Jesus in deeds of love and mercy. All of these can take place not as human possibilities but as works wrought in us by the almighty hand of God. Scriptural holiness means simply "loving the Lord our God with all our heart, and serving him with all our strength." Wesley says along this line:

> Now is it possible for any who believe the Scripture to deny one tittle of this? You cannot. You dare not. You would not for the world. You know it is the pure Word of God. And this is the whole of what we preach. This is the height and depth of what we (with St. Paul) call perfection—a state of soul devoutly to be wished for by all who have tasted of the love of God. O pray for it without ceasing. It is the one thing you want. 'Come with boldness to the throne of grace,' and be assured that when you ask this of God you shall have the 'petition you ask of him.' We know indeed that 'to man'—to the natural man—'this is impossible.' But we know also that as 'no work is impossible with God,' so 'all things are possible to him that believeth' (*Works,* Vol. 11, p. 67).

Here again we see how important faith is. The word *believe* here means faith: the divinely given trust in God's empowering grace through Jesus Christ. In his sermon entitled "The Scripture Way of Salvation," Wesley asks, "But what is that faith whereby we are sanctified, saved from sin and perfected in love?" He answers:

> It is a divine evidence and conviction, first, that God hath promised it in the Holy Scripture. Till we are thoroughly satisfied of this there is no moving one step farther. . . .
> It is a divine evidence and conviction, secondly, that what God hath promised he is *able* to perform. Admitting therefore that 'with men it is impossible' to bring a clean thing out of an unclean, to purify the heart from all sin, and to fill it with all holiness, yet this creates no difficulty in the case, seeing 'with God all things are possible.' And surely no one ever imagines it

was possible to any power less than that of the Almighty! But if God speaks, it shall be done. God saith, 'Let there be light: and there is light' (*Works,* Vol. 2, pp. 167-68).

For Wesley, this went back not only to scripture but also to his own experience. I have in mind his experience the evening of May 24, 1738 when, at a little chapel on Aldersgate Street in London, he "felt his heart strangely warmed." We recall that, during his ministry in Georgia and immediately following it, he felt pangs of spiritual agony. Though he had tried hard to obey God's commandments, he failed often; and somehow he felt that in his spiritual life there was an aching void. His faith was not fixed on Christ (see *Journal,* Vol. 1, pp. 470-72). At Aldersgate something of great importance happened. In addition to the reference to his warmed heart, he said, "I felt I did trust in Christ, Christ alone for salvation; and an assurance was given me that He had taken away *my* sins, even *mine,* and saved *me* from the law of sin and death" (*Journal,* Vol. 1, p. 476).

John Wesley knew well the historic theories of the atoning work of Christ. But now he was aware that Christ was not only the Savior of the world but of *him.* What was the result? He said that previous to this experience he was sometimes, if not often, conquered; "now, I was always conqueror" (*Journal,* Vol. 1, p. 477). In addition, as Maldwyn Edwards says,

> All that had happened in Wesley's life spiritually before 1738 did not produce the dramatic consequences which were brought about by the events which took place on Aldersgate Street. . . .
>
> Until May 24, 1738, Wesley always spoke of what he was doing for God, but after Aldersgate he always spoke of what God was doing for him. Until his conversion, his religious life, though disciplined and earnest, brought no ease of spirit or peace of mind ("The Significance of Aldersgate Today," Nashville: Methodist Evangelistic Materials, n.d., p. 2).

Maldwyn Edwards goes on to say, "Previously he carried his religion, but now his religion carried him" (p. 9).

We see clearly that, according to Wesley, holiness is **not a human achievement but a divine inflowing of the grace of God centered in Christ.** This grace of God flows through channels as the Holy Spirit moves us on the scriptural way toward holiness. According to the Bible, these channels are: prevenient grace, justification, the new birth, and sanctification.

Prevenient Grace

Though this term is not found in the Bible, the reality of it is there. Literally, it means the grace that goes before a conscious repentance and faith in Christ. Wesley called it "preventing grace." Here of course the word does not mean "stopping," or "standing in the way of," but "going before." As we have seen, Wesley strongly affirmed that our human nature in its fallen state is fatally flawed and subject to God's wrath or displeasure. But Wesley believed also that in everyone there is something which makes it possible to respond to God. There is some good in everyone. He knew and appreciated the noble qualities and masterful writings of some of the ancient Greeks and Romans. He appreciated the character of Socrates who said that he must obey God rather than humankind. But he attributed this to the presence of the Spirit in him (*Explanatory Notes Upon the New Testament*, Acts 4:19). As Wesley says,

> If we take this [our salvation] in its utmost extent it will include all that is wrought in the soul by what is frequently termed 'natural conscience,' but more properly, 'preventing grace'; and all the 'drawings' of 'the Father,' the desires after God, which, if we yield to them, increase more and more; all that 'light' wherewith the Son of God 'enlighteneth everyone that cometh into the world,' *showing* every man 'to do justly, to love mercy, and to walk humbly with his God'; all the *convictions* which his Spirit from time to time works in every child of man. Although it is true the generality of men stifle them as soon as possible, and after a while forget, or at least deny, that ever they had them at all (*Works*, Vol. 2, pp. 156-57).

Wesley insists that "there is no man that is in a state of mere nature; there is no man, unless he has quenched the Spirit, that is wholly void of the grace of God." Here again Wesley goes on to say that our 'natural conscience' is "more properly termed 'preventing grace'" (*Works*, Vol. 3, p. 207). And this goes back to scripture where we read of "the true light that enlightens every man" (John 1:9), and of the law "written on their hearts" (Rom. 2:15). Against the "Calvinist supposition "that a natural man is *as dead as a stone,*" he wrote of "the utter falseness and absurdity of it, seeing no man living is without some preventing grace" (*Letters,* Vol. VI, p. 239).

In the light of Wesley's teaching on prevenient grace, we may say that the first step toward holiness is taken when we understand that all these "drawings" toward God are the action of the Spirit wooing us to Christ. For then we will not dismiss them or resist them but let the Spirit move us on to God. It is the Spirit who convicts us, who knocks on the door of our hearts, and who pleads with us—unless we resist—to let the savior enter and bring the gift of eternal life.

Justification

This word comes from the law courts. In the New Testament it means God's mighty act of pardoning all our sins, through no merit of our own but through the merits of Jesus Christ who acted on the cross to save us from our sins. Therefore, this marvelous act of God's forgiving grace is made available through faith in Jesus Christ who suffered and died that all our sins might be forgiven. This faith is a gift of the Holy Spirit who thus enables us to rely not upon any merit in ourselves but to trust *wholly* in the Savior. Augustus Toplady summarized this in his hymn, "Rock of Ages":

> Could my tears forever flow,
>   Could my zeal no languor know,
> Those for sin could not atone;
>   Thou must save, and thou alone.
> In my hand no price I bring;
>   Simply to thy cross I cling.
>   (*Book of Hymns,* No. 120)

At the moment when we have this faith we are as pure and holy as a newborn babe. **Justification, then, is the actual beginning of holiness** (cf. Rom. 3:21-26; see also Wesley's sermon entitled, "Justification by Faith," in *Works,* Vol. 1, p. 189).

And the divine revelation which moves us to the savior is the amazing truth that long before we thought of God, God thought of us. As Paul said, "But God shows his love for us in that while we were yet sinners Christ died for us. Since, therefore, we are now justified by his blood, much more shall we be saved by him from the wrath of God" (Rom. 5:8-9; see also 1 John 4:19). Charles Wesley expressed this beautifully when he wrote:

> O Love divine, what hast thou done!
> Th' incarnate God hath died for me!
> The Father's coeternal Son
> Bore all my sins upon the tree!
> The Son of God for me hath died:
> My Lord, my Love, is crucified!
> (*Book of Hymns*, No. 420)

The New Birth

Wesley believed that at the very moment when God pardons us (justifies us) we are "born of the Spirit" through the redemption in Jesus Christ ("The New Birth" in *Works*, Vol. 2, p. 187). This too is made possible by faith alone. What is this new birth? Just as a baby is born at a moment—or in a relatively short time—so it is with our spiritual birth. When we are pardoned (God's act *for* us), God acts *in* us to recreate our souls. We become new creations in Christ. "The old has passed away, behold the new has come" (2 Cor. 5:17).

John Wesley's great passion was to help people see and realize that *the "inward principle" is the heart of true Christianity.* That is, he believed that unless the *inner life* of a human being is transformed, nothing much has happened. Without this new creation, religion is reduced to talk without the power over temptation and sin. It is form without substance (see 1 Cor. 4:19-20; 2 Tim. 3:5). This new birth is necessary. As Jesus said to Nicodemus, "You must be born anew" (John 3:7). We may follow the forms and ceremonies of religion and not have the substance of it. We may do many good things, which have their place, and still not be right with God. Paul expressed this in the strongest terms when he said, "And if I have prophetic powers, and understand all mysteries and all knowledge, and if I have all faith, so as to remove mountains, but have not love, I am nothing" (1 Cor. 13:2-3).

What is this new birth? It is inner holiness. Old things have passed away. All things have become new: a new awareness of God's continuing presence in our souls, new aims or goals, new appreciation of others (beginning in our families and with those closest to us), new at titudes, new ways of using time, new habits, new moral standards and values, new pocketbooks, new involvement in the church (the Body of Christ), a new awareness of being a child of God and belonging in his kingdom, a new passion for justice and peace in a war-torn and suffering world, and a new sense of destiny under the lordship of Jesus Christ.

As Wesley says,

> It is that great change which God works in the soul when he brings it into life; when he raises it from the death of sin to the life of righteousness. It is the change wrought in the whole soul by the almighty Spirit of God when it is 'created anew in Christ Jesus,' when it is 'renewed after the image of God,' 'in righteousness and true holiness,' when the love of the world is changed into the love of God, pride into humility, passion into meekness; hatred, envy, malice, into a sincere, tender, disinterested love for all mankind ("The New Birth" in *Works*, Vol. 2, pp. 193-94).

Wesley says of the new birth that it is "a vast inward change; a change wrought in the soul by the operation of the Holy Ghost, a change in the whole manner of our existence" (*Works*, Vol. 1, p. 432).

Sanctification

The new birth is the doorway to sanctification. It is the start of that "inward holiness" which leads to "outward holiness." Therefore sanctification is the principle of growth toward "Christian perfection."

Another teaching of Wesley on sanctification which needs to be mentioned here is his idea of instantaneous sanctification. Wesley says that God acts in a moment to elevate the soul to be truly perfect in its love for God and neighbor. He says further that in most people, when this happens, it does so shortly before death. In addition, Wesley says that we should be very careful about speaking on instantaneous sanctification because in many circles it is easily misunderstood (see his "A Plain Account of Christian Perfection," in *Works* (Z), XI, p. 388; see also *Works* (Z), VIII, pp. 296-97). Wesley never claimed this experience for himself.

In any event, his primary emphasis was on **sanctification as the passionate, determined pursuit—with the assistance of the Holy Spirit—of "inward holiness" that leads to "outward**

holiness." And this begins, continues, and reaches toward fulfillment *by grace through faith.* *

What are the fruits of this "inward holiness"? What is the meaning of "outward holiness"? Wesley says that it means two things: works of piety and works of mercy. Works of piety concern the regular involvement in the stated means of grace. For the inner life must be spiritually nurtured with great care. This, in turn, means the active practice of private devotions, meditation, study, and responsiveness to God's Word in the Bible. In addition, it means regular involvement with other Christians in public worship, in the sacrament of Holy Communion, and in the fellowship of believers. The fruit of the Spirit resulting from this cultivation of the inner life was identified by Paul as: "love, joy, peace, patience, kindness, goodness, faithfulness, gentleness, self-control" (Gal. 5:22-23). Wesley makes much of the change of our "temper" and of freedom from pride, envy, malice, an unforgiving spirit, and bad attitudes generally.

Works of mercy are all those deeds of every kind which are of help to others in need, beginning at home and among fellow-members of the united societies and reaching out to any and all people in need—our neighbors. For Wesley this sphere of "outward holiness" implies a determined or sustained alertness to the physical and spiritual needs of people and the will to act in their behalf. For "inward holiness" means seeing others through the eyes of Christ and therefore responding to the needs of others as Jesus did. (For one of Wesley's finest statements on this experienced "inward principle" and its direct effect on our action, see *Works*, Vol. 11, pp. 258-59.)

Wesley's teachings have vast implications concerning what scriptural holiness means. In our effort to see what scriptural holiness means today, we shall be careful to bear in mind the biblical guidelines as interpreted by Wesley.

---

*In the light of Wesley's teaching on scriptural holiness, we can see why he felt that both predestinarianism and antinomianism were enemies of holiness. Predestinarianism shuts the door by placing our salvation in God's hands without any inward response and change in us. Antinomianism relies on God's grace without hearing God's call to obey his commandments.

CHAPTER FIVE

SCRIPTURAL HOLINESS FOR US TODAY

What Holiness Is Not

e begin, as Wesley did, by saying what inward holiness is not. Wesley made it clear that Christian perfection or holiness is not freedom from ignorance, or from mistakes, or from misunderstandings, or from problems, or from temptations, or from the possibility of slowly ignoring or rejecting God's grace. Again, it is not a fixed state precluding growth in grace. What else is it not?

Scriptural holiness is not anything that is merely psychological. Without denying the place of psychology, holiness is not wholeness of personality and of bodily health, though it tends to produce these. It is not emotional balance and healing, though, again, it tends to bring these. Similarly, it is not personality integration, though this comes from it. It is not positive thinking, though it leads to that. It is not possibility thinking, though it surely quickens the imagination to seek nobler possibilities of life and service. Why is it not any of these? Because these do not come to focus on the holy God who has revealed himself and made his grace available through Jesus Christ. The unique dimension of grace is missing. Grace has been defined as God's action in us. But this lacks the specificity which we find in the New Testament. Of course God acts in us, for us, and around us. If God were to cease acting in us and for us, we would instantly perish. The grace of God moving us toward holiness is the *presence and power of God in Jesus Christ through the working of the Holy Spirit*. For it is this which floods our souls with the love of God and neighbor.

Again, holiness is not aesthetic experience, even though the enjoyment of beautiful things is very dear to all who love God. Satisfying

45

experiences through sight, sound, odor, taste, and touch have their importance in God's creation. But holiness is different from these. It is possible to be a connoisseur of art, music, literature, and taste, and be very far removed from holiness.

Further still, scriptural holiness is not goal setting, resolution making, strategy planning, though these may be among its fine results. It is not moral activity of any kind, or merely moral action to help others. These as surely follow upon it as the night follows the day. But it is different from the merely ethical life. For ethics without God are man-made; and holiness is God-made. For this reason one may be an expert in ethical theory and in understanding justice, peacemaking, and good will and not experience holiness. Yet all of these excellent results become a growing outcome of holiness.

Implied in the ethical realm is the concern for human dignity and human rights. I know of few areas pertaining to human existence on this planet more important than this. However laudable this passion for human rights should be, it is not the same as the passion to let God weave into our lives divine holiness, which then motivates our works of mercy. Moreover, we may be thinking so much about human dignity and rights as to lose sight of what is necessary for holiness, for Christian perfection. The unfathomable mystery of iniquity may be ignored so persistently and blindly in human beings as to lead us to miss what may be most needed for people to rise to the life of dignity and honor. Few things are further from scriptural holiness than sentimental assessments of human nature.

Again, holiness is not to be identified with common civilities, politeness, and cultural refinement. These are important, and, generally, they will be among the sure fruits of holiness. Emerson said that the mark of a truly cultured person is that everyone feels at home in his/her presence. This, like humor and morality, is akin to holiness. But here again, the sense of the need for God and the longing for God's righteousness goes far beyond our common civilities and refinements.

Holiness is not the study and understanding of the Bible and Christian beliefs, even though there is no true holiness for us without these. Intellectual contemplation, though worthy and important in the growing Christian life, is not in itself scriptural holiness. For even the intellectual quest for important truths may not be motivated by the desire to please God and receive the bountiful resources of divine grace.

Holiness is not having a good sense of humor, though the ability to see the humor of life situations and to laugh at oneself is close to it. The quest for humor is one thing, the quest for God is another.

Even in certain experiences where God is at work, holiness may be only minimally present. Holiness is not the mystical vision of God, or the feeling of being absorbed into the divine Being. Holiness is not confined to those who may receive special gifts of the Spirit. Holiness is not speaking in tongues. For speaking in tongues is confined to a few, and holiness is for everyone. Moreover, tongues may be like a "noisy gong or a clanging cymbal." And they will pass away. Holiness is not the gift of healing, though this may come from the Holy Spirit. It is not giving money and expecting to gain prosperity. There is nothing holy about that, though God is pleased to see us prosper honorably whenever we can. Holiness is not the gift of foretelling events. Nor is it the gift of discerning "spirits" or situations.

Moreover, in relation to each of these things which may be mistaken for holiness there is the danger that it will function in us as a distraction, turning us away from holiness. For example, if we are looking toward psychological benefits, we may never consider praying for and seeking holiness. Or, if we see and feel the glory of aesthetic experiences, holiness may be pushed aside or totally ignored under the illusion that aesthetic experience is a substitute for God's grace.

So is it with our ethical life. Our moral nature is a great blessing. But we may be so concerned about what *we* can do as good moral people that we become blind to the holiness which comes from God. And even the struggle for human rights—though laudable and to be encouraged—may take up so much of our attention as to cause us to lay aside the passion for holiness. Similarly, the human intellect is one of God's grand gifts to us. But intellectual contemplation—even of lofty topics—may lure us aside from holiness.

In our activity on behalf of the church itself, we may become so pleased with ourselves that we forget about God's call to inner holiness. Again, we may become so obsessed with climbing the ladder to behold the vision of God or to become so absorbed in a mystical union with God as to withdraw from the world and miss the way to true holiness. Or we may be so fascinated with speaking in tongues, or being healed, or becoming prosperous, or predicting events, that we cannot remember when we last felt the need of God's holiness or when we last thought of God's righteousness. Once more, we may feel so good when we praise God and magnify his holy name that we are deaf to God's call to integrity and righteousness. Why is not holiness any of these things? Because, again, they do not in and of themselves lead us to seek the promised "power from on high" and to connect that power with our God-given mission.

Therefore, while recognizing that the experiences and activities mentioned in the foregoing paragraphs may have a place, we see that they are different from the passionate yearning for that holiness which flows into our souls through the grace of God in Jesus Christ our Savior and flows out into the lives of others.

What Holiness Is

What then is holiness as taught in the Bible and in Wesley's understanding of the Bible? Holiness is loving God with all your heart, soul, mind, and strength, and loving your neighbor as yourself (Mark 12:30-31; Matt. 22:35-39). These words are easy to say but hard to do. In fact, we cannot obey these two royal commandments without the grace of God. What is the meaning of the words, "with all your heart, soul, mind, and strength"? We begin to understand them when we read what Jesus said before using them. He said, "Hear O Israel: The Lord our God, the Lord is one" (Mark 12:29). Before considering the commandments, we are to fix our minds and hearts prayerfully on the One who gives the commands. God is our God. And God alone is the Creator and Lord of our lives. The Lord our God, the pure and Holy One, alone has the ultimate and unqualified claim upon our lives. Not only did he give us life in the first place, but long before we thought of God, he took the initiative in Jesus Christ to provide for our salvation. Our God did not wait for us to come to him. He acted through our crucified Savior out of his boundless love for us because he did not want us to perish but to have everlasting life.

Therefore, our God calls for total commitment from *all* that we are or ever hope to become. Love for God, loyalty to God, absolute trust in our holy God—these cannot be divided into fractions. We cannot truly love God 50 percent, or 90 percent, or even 99 percent. Love and loyalty are absolute. In addition, though we fall short, the word *all* means that we are to love God in and with every aspect of our being and energy. This in turn means that since God is holy, we are to seek God's righteousness. We are to pray that it becomes in us a "well of water springing up into everlasting life." It means that we are to be open and receptive to God's inflowing love and to respond in faith to God's leading with all our heart, soul, mind, and strength. The words *heart, soul, mind,* and *strength* refer to our total selfhood or being, to all of our capacities and all that we are. They include our emotions, our will, our imagination, our intellect, our hopes, our possessions, our interpersonal relations. Those words include our adoration and praise to God and imply our gratitude for all God has done for us. And in expressing their meaning we sing, "Take my life, and let it be consecrated, Lord, to thee."

Jesus taught us to love God with **all our mind**. To love God is not to lapse into stupidity or to abandon our God-given common sense. For the scholars in our midst, this means serving the God of all truth by the passionate pursuit and communication of truth. For all Christians this means serving God with the best use of our practical intelligence. And for all of us it means ever growing in understanding God's holy Word and purpose for the children of God.

Our total being and our total network of possessions and relationships are required. This love for God flows into us through the presence of the living Christ. It becomes in us the grand dynamic power of God flowing in us and through us like an everlasting stream toward the kingdom of God and his righteousness. When this love of God in Christ is sustained and nurtured, our continuing prayer—the greatest of all prayers—becomes:

> Thy kingdom come,
> Thy will be done,
> On earth as it is in heaven.

This absolute love of God leads us—motivates and drives us—to love our neighbor as ourselves. This means that we pray and strive to see others as God sees them. God knows their sins and failures as well as ours. But God still loves them and us. God is not pleased with everything about any of us, but he longs to draw us all into his everlasting arms of love. Therefore, we are to pray for and promote God's best for everyone. Jesus set the perfect standard here when he said, "A new commandment I give you, that you love one another; even as I have loved you, that you also love one another. By this all men will know that you are my disciples, if you have love for one another" (John 13:34-35).

How Do We Move Toward Holiness?

How does holiness begin in us? It begins in all those yearnings within us for God which lead us to that response to God in faith which is the new birth. Then, by the grace of God, it grows as long as we live on earth and into the everlasting life in heaven. Let us consider now in some detail what this beginning and continuing in grace means.

Strange as it may seem, holiness begins when we recognize our deepseated moral and spiritual needs. This is the opposite of all easygoing self-approval or smugness. We must never lose sight of the deepseated difficulties in human nature. As Wesley said, those difficulties are to be found not merely in some aspect of human nature, or in particular vices (which are symptomatic of the deeper difficulty), but pervasively throughout. There is no area of human life which is not subject to corruption from pride, self-centeredness, envy, jealousy, lust, greed, resentment, vengeance, ingratitude, unkindness, a bad spirit, bad words and conversations, laziness, misuse of time and energy, distractions, and above all, ignoring our Creator, Sustainer, and Redeemer as though God's holy summons and commandments were of no account. The humble, prayerful, sorrowful recognition of this is the real beginning of the movement toward holiness. For without this, by a kind of gravitational pull, we lapse into complacency or even defiance of God and his claims. Therefore we need to linger upon this theme long enough for the awesome nature of our problem to be seen and felt.

Plato saw something of this when he likened human nature to a charioteer trying to drive two horses which are yoked together, one of which is unruly and the other of which is trained and responsive to the charioteer.

The French epigrammatic moralist, La Rochefoucauld (1613-1680) spoke of our self-love as "one long and mighty agitation." Pascal (1623-1662) said that human beings are "incapable both of truth and of good." Schopenhauer (1788-1860), the grand pessimist, said, "It seems to me that the idea of dignity can be applied only in an ironical sense to a being whose will is so sinful, whose intellect is so limited, whose body is so weak and perishable as man's." And William Hazlitt (1778-1830), who was one of the keenest observers of human nature, declared that "envy is the most universal passion."

Kant (1724-1804) said that there is a "radical evil" in human nature.

After long reflection on the human scene, Hegel (1770-1831) said that history is "the slaughter-bench at which the happiness of peoples, the wisdom of states, and the virtue of individuals have been victimized." Our own Josiah Royce (1855-1916) wrote significant words on this theme. Instead of calling it "original sin," he identified this reality as the "moral burden of the individual." In a moment of insight rather rare among philosophers, he said,

> The individual human being is by nature subject to some over-whelming moral burden from which, if unaided, he cannot escape. Both because of what has technically been called original sin, and because of the sins that he himself has committed, the individual is doomed to a spiritual ruin from which only a divine intervention can save him (*The Problem of Christianity*, p. 100).

Does it not seem strange that in our time an outstanding psychiatrist would be urging our sophisticated society to face the fact of sin? (See Karl Menninger, *Whatever Became of Sin?*.) And does it not make us stop and think, in this age of enlightenment, when a Harvard psychiatrist, Dr. Robert Coles, suggests that, through direct contact with children and common folk, he has found his way back to the Sermon on the Mount? For out of his experiences with the poor, he learned that, as Jesus said, what matters most comes not from without—the circum-stances of life—but from what is in the heart of an individual man, woman, or child.

There seems to be a kind of determined self-deception which causes modern humans to turn off the light on the depths of our moral and spiritual sickness. This is what happened in Wesley's day when the deists and the apostles of the Enlightenment refused to take sin seriously. Is it the smug belief in a cultural evolution which is slowly moving us toward paradise? Is it the belief that there is something good about saying that everyone is accepted, regardless of how sorry he or she is? Is it the illusion that education and science and technology will solve all our problems? Reinhold Niebuhr may be right when he says,

> The whole structure of the modern interpretation of life and history was, in short, a very clever contrivance of human pride to obscure the weakness and insecurity of man; of the human con-science to hide the sin into which men fall through their efforts to

override their weakness and insecurity; and of human sloth to evade responsibility (*Faith and History*, p. 99).

One would think that two World Wars, Korea, Vietnam, Iran-Iraq, Central America, South Africa, the awesome drug scene—including alcohol—pervasive dishonesty in government and in financial matters, sexual promiscuity and perversions, pollution of the environment, the threat of nuclear destruction, the wasteland on TV—that all this and numerous other evils and problems would wake us up to see our urgent need for the grace of God which alone produces holiness. But, alas, our blindness clings to us like a chronic malady. Modern human beings seem to confront a future—an eschatology—of fear and despair, without God and without hope.

The depths of our situation as creatures of profound moral and spiritual needs are not reached until we move into the biblical teaching. Only the divine revelation can break through the hard crust of our pride, selfishness, and cheap excuses. It is not until we see ourselves in the light of the holy God who made us to be his faithful children that we see ourselves as we really are. This profound disturbing revelation on our human nature can be seen in all its depths because God has revealed also that his love for us is unfailing. But God will not allow us to drift into the easy conscience merely because we know he loves us. For the "wrath of God" is real, and it is to be taken with utmost seriousness. God's love is never to be seen in separation from his justice. In the light of the biblical faith we are required to face the monstrous dimensions of our sin and failure because we can hold before us the profounder reality of God's love and of God's marvelous deliverance through Jesus Christ. For there we encounter the God who throws his light upon the reality and evil character of sin and upon the grace which overcomes it. For where sin abounded, grace abounded all the more (Rom. 5:20).

But God has provided for our deliverance from bondage to all that wrong living which displeases God who made us for his righteousness. Wesley called it "The Scripture Way of Salvation" (Sermon No. 43 in *Works*, Vol. 2, pp. 155-69). Where there is no bondage, there is no need for deliverance. Where there is bondage and no answer to it, there is either bitter despair and disillusionment or the desperate plunge into distractions and false answers. Where there is the recognition of bondage and the revealed vision of God's answer to it in Jesus Christ, we can pass from death to life by faith. For we can walk with God in the assurance that he will move us toward that holiness for which he created us. We do not require God's grace for sorry living.

As we have seen, Wesley insisted that true Christianity is the religion of the heart. The "inner principle" was so basic in Wesley and in the evangelical revival under Wesley that I must refer to it again in his own words:

> Do some of you ask: "But dost thou acknowledge *the inward principle?*" I do, my friends; and I would to God every one of you acknowledged it as much. I say, all religion is either *empty show*, or *perfection by inspiration*; in other words, the obedient love of God by the supernatural knowledge of God. Yea, and that all which "is not of faith is sin"; and which does not spring from this loving knowledge of God, which knowledge cannot begin, or subsist one moment, without *immediate inspiration*; not only all public worship, and all private prayer, but every thought, in common life, and word and work. What think you of this? Do you not stagger? Dare you carry *the inward principle* so far? Do you acknowledge it to be the very truth? But alas! what is the acknowledging it? Dost thou experience this principle in thyself? What saith thy heart? Does God dwell therein? And doth it now echo to the voice of God? Hast thou the *continual inspiration* of his Spirit filling thy heart with his love, as with 'a well of water springing up into everlasting life'? (*Works*, Vol. 11, p. 258).

In the light of the awful realities of our sinful nature and life, our only hope is to recover with Wesley the apostolic confidence in the power of God—through the Holy Spirit—to change us, recreate us, and empower us for victory over temptation and sin and for service to God and neighbor. We must see that the living Christ in us is greater than the sum total of all our sins and failures. And, seeing this, we must hold fast to the Savior who is able to save to the uttermost. This faith will lead us also to be receptive to the pentecostal inflowing of the Holy Spirit through whom we are empowered *for* mission and *in* mission.

The Bible makes it transparently clear that God is not overcome by our burdens and sins. God is unutterably greater than all the forces of evil in the world. Therefore, we are to join the apostles in experiencing that lifegiving faith whereby we become more than conquerors through Christ who loved us (Rom. 8:37). How, then, is it possible to obey God's call to holiness? By grace through faith. But we must be sure to know that this grace of God is no mere struggling, trickling stream. On the contrary, as Paul knew, in Christ it is the "power of God for salvation to everyone who believes." And as the apostles and others knew at Pentecost, it is the empowerment for carrying out God's mission in the world.

The Fruit of Scriptural Holiness

The inspired writers remind us again and again of the fruit of this righteousness from above. As Paul said, "the fruit of the Spirit is love, joy, peace, patience, kindness, goodness, faithfulness, gentleness, self-control; against such there is no law" (Gal. 5:22-23). In the call to scriptural holiness we hear and feel the divine impulse to become agents of reconciliation, beginning at home. We create an atmosphere in which people in society can breathe. And, by grace, we stand and work with others in every worthy cause in which we can make a contribution.

Another fruit of scriptural holiness is commitment to the stewardship of our bodies, our souls, our talents, our time, our money and possessions, that God may be glorified and human beings liberated from whatever holds them in bondage. This means the building up of the good people and forces in community life, including government, education, family life, entertainment, mass media, and in business and labor. Because of God's grace, scriptural holiness motivates us to concentrate our energies sufficiently to bring about changes wherever we can. We labor with others in the struggle for peace and justice. Whatever harms the bodies and souls of people becomes our enemy. And whatever builds people up and helps them to rise above poverty, disease, and ignorance becomes our ally.

Scriptural holiness motivates us to do what we can to help the homeless, the hungry, the sick throughout the world. It moves us also to encourage and promote the development of minds, talents, and skills of children, youth, and adults. All of these are among the great areas of human need.

Scriptural holiness leads to an understanding of God's revealed plan of salvation. And we are led to know that this has top priority with God. God's plan is to redeem people through Jesus Christ and his church. Therefore, a major fruit of scriptural holiness is the sustained desire to draw others whom we know to Jesus Christ and to lead them into the Christian life through the community of prayer, faith, and service. One of the most important fruits of holiness is the passion to respond to our Risen Lord's summons to "go and make disciples." For there is within us the concern for lost souls, that they might not perish but have eternal life (John 3:16).

Once more, by the grace of God leading us toward scriptural holiness, one of the best and most beautiful fruits of that holiness is the presence on this astonishing little planet of truly noble souls who walk with the Lord.

The Rewards of Scriptural Holiness

The rewards of scriptural holiness are almost beyond words. But some effort must be made to recount them. The Bible is often a book containing "If . . . then" statements, especially when speaking of holiness. For example, if we love God and obey God, numberless blessings follow. If not, disaster. Our primary reason for seeking holiness is to glorify God and be a blessing to our fellow human beings. But God, in his infinite love and wisdom, allows many blessings to those who love and serve him. This is why Jesus said, "But seek first his kingdom and his righteousness, and all these things shall be yours as well" (Matt. 6:33). The kingdom has priority, but the blessings do follow.

It may sound pious to say that we are to become Christians without any regard for the rewards. But this is not essentially biblical. The person who "walks not in the counsel of the wicked, nor stands in the way of sinners" is "blessed," truly happy (Ps. 1:1). In every one of the Beatitudes (Matt. 5:3-11), Jesus promised a reward. And the rewards are priceless. To the poor in spirit will belong the kingdom of heaven. Those who mourn and are sorry for their sins will be comforted. The meek—who are strong spiritually—will inherit the earth. For, as John Wesley puts it,

> How beauteous nature now!
> How dark and sad before!
> With joy we view the pleasing change,
> And nature's God adore.
> (*Book of Hymns*, No. 492)

Those who truly hunger and thirst for righteousness will be filled. The merciful will receive mercy. The pure in heart will see God. Who else? The peacemakers will be called the children of God. Those who are persecuted in good causes will be in the kingdom of heaven. And those who do not return evil for evil, when persecuted and lied about, are to rejoice because their "reward is great in heaven."

Scriptural holiness means waking up in the morning with a song in our hearts because of the marvelous gift of life for another day (See Ps. 118:24). It means **a positive, adventurous, creative spirit**. For constant negative thinking, like other sins, undermines the spiritual life. Scriptural holiness leads to the "peace of God which passes all understanding" (Phil. 4:7)—not as the world gives. There will be the inward flow of joy, the experience of sins forgiven, a clear conscience, the victory over temptation, the power over canceled sin, the freedom from bondage. Scriptural holiness means the glory of gratitude to God, the wonderful sense of adoration and praise, the sustained will to love other people, and God's approval for work well done. This does not mean freedom from tears and tribulations. But it means that even in these we feel the mysterious sustaining and empowering presence of the Holy Spirit who comforts and strengthens us. For we know from experience the all-sufficiency of the grace of God in Christ Jesus (see 2 Cor. 12:9). Again, it means the continuing sense of the presence of the pardoning and gracious Father of us all in and through our day-by-day pilgrimage.

Scriptural holiness yields the rewards of **fellowship** within the church. It means the joy and privilege of intercessory prayer, the sympathetic tear, the mystic union of oneness in the Body of Christ. It means the turning over to God of all those with whom we have family ties, and our consequent deeds in their behalf because we want all the blessings God has for them.

The supreme reward is **heaven** itself. There are many Christians who never think of hell. They feel that somehow God is going to work things out for everyone to go to heaven. I understand this feeling. There are a few passages of scripture which may be used to support it, including the words that "every knee should bow, in heaven and on earth and under the earth, and every tongue confess that Jesus Christ is Lord" (Phil. 2:10-11; cf. Isa. 45:23; Rom. 14:11). These references may be interpreted in quite a different way from the one which implies that all will ultimately be saved. Jesus taught us to take seriously the danger of going to hell. It is interesting to observe that Jesus, who "came that we might have life, and have it more abundantly," had more to say about hell than those who penned the books of the New Testament other than the four Gospels. Jesus warned repeatedly of the judgment of God, and spoke of the time when the sheep would be separated from the goats.

If all are to be saved regardless of their faithlessness and ways of life, Christ came, lived, died, and was raised from the dead in vain. For how could he be the Savior for all when they would ultimately be saved anyway?

It is no small thing to enter into an everlasting life with God and those who love and serve God in heaven. It is no human achievement, but the gift of God through Jesus Christ who died to save us from our sins. This is what God has revealed to us regarding our future beyond death. God has made it clear in the Bible that we are not immortal by nature, but we attain everlasting life by grace through faith. And this life everlasting begins here and now, on earth. It is in the light of the biblical revelation on the life everlasting that we hold fast to Jesus Christ who gave himself to pardon us and to lift us up to the life eternal in that heavenly kingdom which has been prepared for human beings from the foundation of the world. Therefore, **it makes all the difference between heaven and hell as to whether or not we live by faith in the Son of God and bear the fruits of faith**. "How shall we escape if we neglect such a great salvation?" (Heb. 2-3).

It is partly because of the lively hope of the reward of heaven that we must do all we can, as long as we have breath, to glorify God and serve him through deeds of love and mercy. Thus Paul could say, following his inspired remarks on the victory over sin and death, "Therefore, my beloved brethren, be steadfast, immovable, always abounding in the work of the Lord, knowing that in the Lord your labor is not in vain" (1 Cor. 15:58).

The rewards are indeed great both in this life and in the life to come. Therefore, we are to hear each day the call of the Holy God to "strive for peace with all men, and for the holiness without which no one will see the Lord" (Heb. 12:14).

CHAPTER SIX

SCRIPTURAL HOLINESS AND OUR CHRISTIAN AFFECTIONS

hen we love God with all our heart, soul, mind, and strength, and love our neighbor as ourselves, our whole life is transformed. In this chapter we are to see how our affections—our feelings and emotions—are elevated and purified by God's grace in Jesus Christ. In addition, we shall see how they function in the total movement of our souls in our life with God. In particular, we shall consider five Christian affections which reach their highest levels by the grace of God through faith. As we shall see, these are so mysteriously intermingled with the ongoing processes in our spiritual pilgrimage that they move us toward scriptural holiness and, at the same time, are produced by it.

These five Christian affections are: (1) the feeling of absolute *dependence* on God which moves us to the lifegiving faith in Jesus Christ as our personal Savior and Lord; (2) the sense of *belonging* to God's family (assurance) as a direct consequence of that faith; (3) the sustained feeling of *gratitude* to God from whom all blessings flow; (4) the inner flow of joy, praise, and *adoration;* and (5) the *compassionate concern* for others which is born and nurtured by grace through faith. We shall consider these in that order. But two important reminders are necessary.

The Source of Our Affections

The first reminder is that each of these Christian affections comes directly out of our understanding of God which has been revealed in the Bible, and supremely in Jesus Christ. Where there are no great realities, there can be no great affections or emotions. There may be excitement—as at an athletic event, or a political convention, or a rock music concert. But these are on a totally different level from the Christian affections.

Our emotions do not just happen apart from their total context. If in the ninth inning of a baseball game a home crowd sees a winning homerun, they express in a spontaneous outburst their feeling of joy because of the reality of the ball going over the fence and the victory which it brings. So is it with a last-minute touchdown in a football game. Why do we feel one thing when we see an ant-hill and have a vastly different feeling when we see the Alps? The objective reality produces the feeling. When we read or hear a wonderful succession of poetic words, our affections well up within us. Again, it is the events at a wedding ceremony which move us to tears of joy and hope. When a child is born into a home, there is great joy because of the "blessed event." And it is the reality of death that brings us bitter grief and sorrow at a funeral.

Turn to any sphere of life, and we find the same principle at work. The realities awaken, qualify, and produce our affections. If a person secures a desired position, there is a deep sense of joy. If a job is lost, there follows the whole concatenation of emotions from bitterness, to depression, to despair, to emptiness, to loneliness, as well as, eventually, the feeling of anticipation over new possibilities. The plain fact, universally experienced, is that our emotions are produced in their varying kinds and degrees by the realities within and without which are confronted. Those realities may be inner wrongness or rightness, or outer things, or events, or relationships, or various combinations of these.

This same principle applies to our Christian affections. But there is this difference: These affections are on a different level from all others because of the ultimate and absolute nature of the realities involved because of God's initiative and because of our faith in God. Here we are dealing with the relationships between God and human beings. And these are different from all others because they are life, death, and destiny relationships. But beyond these, there is the unique dimension of the religious and, more particularly, the Christian affections. Moreover, by virtue of the realities involved, these Christian affections have a direct bearing on our salvation. And they bring a new glory into all other areas of life. The realities of God, grace, redemption in Christ, illumination, comfort, and empowerment by the Holy Spirit—when accompanied with our response of faith—these *create the Christian affections and set them in motion.*

The second reminder is that these Christian affections are nurtured and sustained through association and fellowship within the community of prayer, faith, and service. To be sure, they are nurtured through private prayer, study, responsive meditation on God's Word, and on our decisions and our faith. Beyond these, God has revealed that it is his holy purpose to work in and through people in communities of prayer, faith, and service. In the Old Testament we see God at work not only in Abraham, Moses, David, and the prophets, but also in the *people of Israel.* In the New Testament we see that Jesus chose the apostles and formed them—despite Judas—into a community which bore his name. At Pentecost, the Holy Spirit bound the followers of Jesus together and strengthened them in their Christian affections through their fellowship of prayer, faith, and service. And Paul went out to the Gentiles to preach and teach the gospel. He went also to bring Christians together into churches.

It was in these communities that the Christian affections became sustained experiences. For there the Apostolic teachings were kept alive from generation to generation. It was there that the Old Testament was held up as scripture. It was there that the story of Jesus was told. And, eventually, it was there that the New Testament was produced and recognized to be the living Word of God.

Holiness and Our Affections

The five major Christian affections have their ultimate source and meaning in relation to the reality, greatness, and glory of God in Jesus Christ and in relation to our response of faith as part of a community.

(1) The first of these affections is the feeling of **absolute dependence on God,** which moves us toward the lifegiving faith in Jesus Christ. In one of Wesley's finest portraits of a Christian (*Works,* Vol. 11, pp. 527-31), he says that a Christian has "a continual sense of his dependence on the Parent of good for his being, and all the blessings that attend it" (p. 527). Incidentally, another of Wesley's portraits of a Christian is in his essay on "The Character of a Methodist" (*Works* (Z), VIII, pp. 340-47).

Incomparably more important than Wesley was Jesus, from whom Wesley derived an emphasis on "real Christianity." We see clearly this focus on Jesus from Wesley's thirteen sermons "Upon our Lord's Sermon on the Mount" (Sermons Nos. 21-33 in *Works*, Vol. 1). Early in Wesley's ministry (1739-1746), the evangelist preached more than a hundred sermons from separate texts in the Sermon on the Mount.

On inward holiness we sit at the feet of Jesus and learn from him. In one of his most beautiful and meaningful Beatitudes, Jesus said, "Blessed are the poor in spirit, for theirs is the kingdom of heaven" (Matt. 5:3). Who are "the poor in spirit"? They are not those who go around rating themselves as lowly or having a "poor-little-me" attitude. Nor are they those who put on airs of humility. "The poor in spirit" are those who, by divine grace, feel their absolute dependence on God. And this affection seems to involve at least three areas of our absolute dependence on God.

(a) First, "the poor in spirit" feel their dependence on God for their very existence. They are aware of God as their Maker or Source. They are aware also that if God's energies were withdrawn from them at any moment, they would instantly perish. Far from their thought is the notion that they are self-made and self-owned. For they are keenly aware that God alone has the ultimate claim upon their bodies, minds, and souls. By divine grace they are given to behold the reality of their bodies and souls in relation to the invisible and eternal God.

(b) Second, "the poor in spirit" feel their need for God's redeeming grace. They are aware of their sin and feel Godly sorrow because they have turned away from the Creator's holy purpose for them. Therefore this feeling of absolute dependence on God contains in it this sorrow over having displeased God. And there is the mysterious and awesome sense of the desperate need for God's forgiving grace through the Savior. Because they know that Christ died for them and that through his merits alone they are forgiven, they feel their continuing need for God's redeeming grace.

(c) Third, "the poor in spirit" know that they cannot be what God created them to be—and what they themselves really want to be—without God's continuing help. They feel the force of the temptations which can make or destroy them. They feel the emotional tugs and pulls away from God's holy purpose for them. They feel the struggle to maintain right attitudes toward others, beginning at home. They feel their need for divine intervention and cry out for God's help. In a word, they feel the need for the "power from on high." And they pray for this empowering presence of the Holy Spirit.

The "poor in Spirit" are, in the truest sense, humble before God and their fellow human beings. For they feel deeply that they and all others stand in the need of prayer and grace. Out of this feeling of absolute dependence on God—and the need for God—comes the saving faith.

As one of the holy affections, this feeling of absolute dependence on God is a primal source of faith, prayer, worship, and service. This Christian affection cannot well up in us unless we see ourselves to be in the presence of the Creator who is absolutely holy and just, and who has taken the initiative to redeem us through Jesus Christ, and to comfort and empower us through the Holy Spirit.

This feeling of absolute dependence on God results in the sense of awe in the presence of God. God is infinite. We are finite. God is the Creator. We are creatures. God is holy. We are sinners. Job experienced this when God confronted him saying, "Where were you when I laid the foundation of the earth?" (Job 38:4). The Psalmist realized this when he prayed, "Whither shall I go from thy Spirit? Or whither shall I flee from thy presence?" (Ps. 139:7). Isaiah felt it when he saw the Lord high and lifted up, whose train filled the temple (Isaiah 6). Paul felt this sense of dependence and awe when he said, "O the depth of the riches and wisdom and knowledge of God! How unsearchable are his judgments and how inscrutable his ways!" (Rom. 11:33).

This feeling of absolute dependence on God reaches its highest level for Christians when we sense ourselves to be in the presence of the *triune* God. For we see ourselves, not only before our Creator and Sustainer. We know ourselves to be in the presence of our Redeemer. We are sinners who feel the need for forgiveness. And just as God alone can create a world, so God the Redeemer alone can pardon our sins. Only the Savior can solve the problem of sin by bringing together the justice and mercy of God. Here our dependence on Christ is absolute.

In addition, we are in the presence of the Holy Spirit who enables us to confess our sins and leads us to the foot of the cross. And there the Spirit helps us to put our faith in God's redeeming grace in Jesus Christ. We feel the need for divine assistance to be what God created us to be. Therefore, we feel our need for God, the Holy Spirit, who is near us and in us. And he draws us mysteriously to Jesus Christ, comforts us, illuminates us, binds us together in Christ, intercedes for us, and empowers us *for* mission and *in* mission.

(2) Second, Christian affection, which is an essential manifestation of holiness, is the sense of **belonging to God and in God's family.** The desire to belong is one of the deepest forces which motivate us. It is basic in our family ties. It gives special meaning to marriage. Friendship, too, is one of the satisfying experiences of our earthly pilgrimage. People long to belong to various kinds of societies and fellowship groups. The popular romantic songs have to do with belonging or not belonging. This universal longing to belong has a profound religious significance. This is the reason belonging to a church, to a Sunday school class, to a pray-study group, to a fellowship of United Methodist Women or United Methodist Men, to a youth group, to a Scout troop, or to other Christian groups has continuing importance.

Holiness produces the sense of belonging in the life of our common humanity. We feel the joys and sorrows of our fellows. And we identify with and long to foster the hopes and dreams of all humankind. And holiness leads us into those mysterious ties of prayer, fellowship, worship, and service which bind us together as Christians.

But deepest of all is the feeling of belonging to God and his kingdom. Holiness—or the true love of God and neighbor—awakened in us by the prior love of God for us, produces through faith this sense of belonging. For thereby we are led to feel that amid all our circumstances, in life and in death, we belong to the God who made us for himself, who has redeemed us by his grace, and who dwells in us, through the Holy Spirit. And we are given the inner witness to know that our heavenly Father, whose nature is love, will never let go of us. We are his, and he is ours. This, in turn, gives meaning and depth to our own sense of kinship with all who are claimed by God and who belong to God.

A special feature of this Christian affection of belonging to God and and in his family is the sense of assurance that our names are "written in the Lamb's book of life." God graciously gives the inner witness. The Holy Spirit bears witness that we have passed from death to life and are now the children of God (Rom. 8:15-16). Therefore, this sense of belonging carries with it the sense of a destiny with God and with all who are faithful.

(3) Holiness leads to gratitude to God and to all who have contributed to our lives. This is one of the grandest of the Christian affections which, again, is born in us by grace through faith. It binds us to God and to our fellow human beings. It is a primal source of the Christian

motivation for service. Luther was once asked why he worked so hard for the Lord. Why all the expenditure of time and energy in translating the Bible, why all the lectures, sermons and letters, and why the struggles for the Protestant Reformation? He replied, "Not all the money in the world could make me do it. But Christ has done so much for me that I have to do everything I can for him."

The psalmists have taught us gratitude to God.

> Give thanks to him, bless his name!
> For the Lord is good;
> His steadfast love endures for ever,
> And his faithfulness to all generations.
> (Ps. 100:4-5)

There was a special formula used by the psalmists and perhaps repeated by the people at public worship:

> O give thanks to the Lord, for he is good;
> for his steadfast love endures forever!
> (Ps. 106:1; 107:1; 118:1,29; 136:1,3;
> cf. 1 Chron. 16:8)

Paul taught the churches to give thanks to God from whom all blessings flow. He was so grateful for what Christ did for him that he lived continuously with the feeling of gratitude. After analyzing the human condition of hopeless bondage, he cried out: "Wretched man that I am! Who will deliver me from this body of death?" Then he said, "Thanks be to God through Jesus Christ our Lord!" (Rom. 7:24-25). This theme of gratitude for victory over sin and death through Jesus Christ was basic with Paul. He gave thanks to God, "who in Christ always leads us in triumph" (2 Cor. 2:14). And he gave thanks for the "inexpressible gift" of the gospel of Christ (2 Cor. 9:13-15). He says, "The sting of death is sin, and the power of sin is the law. But thanks be to God, who gives us the victory through our Lord Jesus Christ" (1 Cor. 15:56-57).

Paul was careful to bring thanksgiving into our daily Christian life. For now we are living every day in Christ. By following the example of Jesus (in Mark 8:6; 14:22; John 6:11), he said we are to give thanks for daily food (1 Tim. 4:3-5). He gave thanks to Prisca and Aquila "who risked their necks" for his life (Rom. 16:3-4). In earnest prayer and supplication we are to be careful to make known our requests to

God *"with thanksgiving"* (Phil. 4:6). Paul took this sense of gratitude so far as to urge the people of Thessalonica to "give thanks *in all circumstances;* for this is the will of God in Christ Jesus for you" (1 Thess. 5:18).

Whether our situations are good or bad, pleasing or distressing, we are to give thanks to God. This does not mean that we are to assume that God would lay upon us the burdens of evil and tragedy. Sometimes the pain and suffering of a situation are so great and so complicated that we can hardly speak, let alone express thanks to God. Of course we are not to "thank God" for such evils that each of us encounters. Yet this pain and suffering are circumstances which can be overcome, given healing and counseling and the love of God and neighbor. The way of scriptural holiness means that, when we truly love God and neighbor, the circumstances of life are secondary. Therefore, in all circumstances, we are to give thanks. For God goes with us into all situations.

(4) Holiness leads to the inner flow of joy, praise, and adoration. This too is one of the Christian affections. When we truly love God and neighbor, there is a well of joy springing up within our souls which leads us to break forth in praise and adoration to God. We want to sing, "Praise God from Whom All Blessings Flow," or "O For a Thousand Tongues to Sing," or "How Great Thou Art!" Or we want to join the psalmist in saying,

> Bless the Lord, O my soul;
> and all that is within me, bless his holy name! (103:1)

Holiness is not this inner flow of joy. But it produces this joy as a God-ordained consequence. For whenever we truly love God and neighbor, there is "the peace of God, which passes all understanding" (Phil. 4:7) and "joy unspeakable and full of glory" (1 Pet. 1:8, KJV).

(5) Holiness, the love of God and neighbor, leads to far more than the recognition that each human being is a creature of value in God's sight. Holiness includes this recognition as a theological base. But it leads to a God-given compassionate concern for others. We are moved to *feel* with our fellow human beings and their needs, their hopes and their dreams. Because Christ lives in us we begin to see others through him. And his great compassion for the suffering and needy people burns in us like a divine flame which sets us on fire to serve others.

We do not *naturally* have this sense of the unutterable preciousness of every human being. But by the mighty power of God's grace at work in us through Jesus Christ, this caring love is born in us. And it reaches out toward all whom we can touch.

This compassionate concern for others is not only an abiding Christian affection; it is a dynamic motivating force within us. For, through Jesus Christ, love becomes the master-impulse of our souls. And this binds us to others in the united effort to minister to the vast ranges of human need.

This Christian affection is nurtured in us more and more as we behold the compassion of Jesus for people—for little children, for lepers, for those with all sorts of diseases and handicapping conditions, for women, men, boys, and girls.

For example, Jesus, in the cumulative influence of his life, has done more to bring dignity to women than all other forces put together. We turn especially to the four Gospels to keep remembering who he was, and what he said and did. We sit at his feet and learn of him. And through him we feel something of his compassion welling up in us and moving us to service.

This Christian affection is no mushy, sentimental, fleeting feeling toward others. For it is based on God's revelation of the preciousness of each human being. And it is nurtured by the grace of God in Christ. The Christian affection, or compassion for others, is no merely human flame lighted from the altars of this world. Rather, it is like a torch lifted high up to the altar of heaven and there lighted with the divine flame of the love of God. It is the sustained desire—born and nurtured in us by grace—for God's best for everyone, including our enemies. As far as our relationships with our fellow human beings are concerned, this is holiness.

CHAPTER SEVEN

SCRIPTURAL HOLINESS IN OUR FAMILY LIFE

 e United Methodists are called of God to spread scriptural holiness over the world. This is our supreme reason for being. But this begins at home. In this chapter we consider the meaning of holiness in our family relationships. It is here, in the intimate face-to-face occasions of daily life that the call to holiness comes to its most personally meaningful expression. As we have seen, holiness is the love of God and neighbor. But this does not go to the heart of holiness unless we understand what the word *love* means.

No Merely Human Affection

The word *love* is used in many senses. Often it is used loosely and flippantly to express relationships which are as far from holiness as hell is from heaven. Sometimes people use the word to express cheap, momentary, and fitful romantic encounters. Sometimes even in religious circles it is used superficially in a kind of casual greeting: "God loves you, and I love you." This may be done in the full measure of sincerity. But it may be said without any intention of devoting oneself to another in times of need. And it may be said with the predominant aim of taking advantage of the sufferings and loneliness of others for selfish gain.

What is scriptural holiness? Or, what is the love of God and neighbor as revealed in the Old and New Testaments? We cannot state strongly enough that holiness is no merely human love. We live in an age of psychological and sociological insight when it is hard to take seriously the transcendent or supernatural dimension of God's grace. Therefore, when we think of love we are apt to look into ourselves and try to identify it in terms of our human feelings of endearment. These affections have their roles to play. But they are not what we have in mind by scriptural holiness or Christian love. Therefore, we must understand clearly and firmly what this Christian love is and the source of this love.

The Nature and Source of Scriptural Holiness

What is this love of God and neighbor as revealed in the New Testament? Christian love is the love which comes through the living Christ in us by the power of the Holy Spirit. Holiness is love produced by the *direct action* of God in us which necessarily issues in deeds of love and mercy. The words *direct action* are critical, for they indicate the immediate presence of the Holy Spirit. In the light of this we see both the nature and source of scriptural holiness. Therefore, we know what we are seeking and how to receive this love as an experienced reality. And of course it is self-evident that we cannot think or speak of scriptural holiness apart from Jesus Christ.

Paul, who gave his earliest and best efforts to an understanding of the religion of the Pharisees, *entered a new dimension of life with God* after the Risen Lord encountered him. He knew it and felt compelled to tell others about it. This is why he could say, "It is no longer I who live, but Christ who lives in me; and the life I live in the flesh I live by faith in the Son of God, who loved me and gave himself for me" (Gal. 2:20). The reality to which Paul gives his testimony here seems far removed from the realms in which most people live out their lives today. But with Paul it was by far the most real, the most important, and the most powerful force he knew. And beyond question he had found the Source of that "more excellent way," of that love of which he wrote in his first letter to the Corinthians (chapter 13).

Wesley experienced this same Source of the power which produces holiness. He too was keenly aware of the *direct action* of Almighty God through Jesus Christ transforming his soul and placing it on a higher plateau of existence.

I do not profess to understand the mystery of Christ in us. I only know that God has acted in Christ and through Christ, by the *direct action* of the Holy Spirit, to fill our souls with the love of God. This is clearly what the New Testament writers are saying. In other words, the Source of scriptural holiness is the immediate presence of God through the Holy Spirit. And it is made available out of the vast supernatural or transcendent resources of God's grace.

By the word *supernatural* I do not mean the superstitious, the occult, the esoteric, the cranky, the illusory, or the fanciful. I mean the realm of grace, of divine energizing beyond God's action throughout the physical universe. I mean the realm of God's grace which is not available through scientific laboratories, or through philosophical reflections, or through theological enterprises, or through concerts, dramas, artworks, travels, athletic events, or through business enterprises, or through skilled or menial labor. All of these are important activities. But they are in different realms from God's boundless grace in Jesus Christ which is made available by faith alone.

Are we any closer to this direct experience of God's love by any external process, or form, or activity? Do we receive this inward holiness by thought, reflection, going to cultural events, or by an extended process of education? Some of these may prepare the way. But Paul and Wesley and millions of other Christians, or saints, as they were known in the New Testament, would tell us that scriptural holiness comes by the *direct action* of the Holy Spirit, that is, by grace through faith.

Holiness in Family Life

Consider what would happen in our homes if we *loved God and others as we love ourselves.*

Holiness would be an empty dream if unrelated to intimate human life. Even the love of God, without the love of neighbor, would lead us into a realm withdrawn from the world and deaf to the cries of suffering human beings. Whatever else Jesus Christ was as the Son of God, he was not permanently withdrawn on some Mount of Temptation, or Mount of Transfiguration. He was God *incarnate*. He withdrew to return to the thick context of struggling, sinful men, women, and children. If Christ is in us, calling and motivating us, where would we begin?

The immediate or direct action of the Holy Spirit moves us to begin where we are. For nearly all people this means beginning in our family situations. Here the primary relationships include persons who are bound with others by blood, adoption, and covenantal commitment. How does scriptural holiness manifest itself in these intimate relationships? Here it is of utmost importance to be both specific and forthright. True holiness—the love of God and neighbor—is always marked by policy decisions. And these involve considerateness, mutual appreciation, and absolute loyalty. Can anyone imagine that we are motivated by the direct action of the Holy Spirit when we are trampling on our solemn promises?

In the ties of matrimony, than which none are more holy, love and loyalty go together. Love without loyalty or fidelity is a contradiction in terms. And those who get themselves involved in extramarital relations may say that they love the one to whom they made their vows, but, before God, they have abused holy love. Nor will any cheap excuses satisfy the kind of love which comes from Christ. The only satisfaction comes through honest repentance and trust in God's forgiving grace—both from God and from those on all sides who have been wronged. And with this there must be the renewed promise and determination to live right with God's help.

There are many ways of trampling upon our love for each other. One is neglect. Another is lack of sincere and continuing appreciation. Another is lying and deceit. Another is by cruel and harsh words. Another is by physical violence. Another is by a judgmental attitude. Another is by constantly reminding each other of past mistakes. Still another is a hardhearted and unforgiving spirit. Who can name all the ways in which people make a mockery of love and loyalty!

The enormous problem of the breakdown in our character means, in the first instance, the loss of our own self-respect. For anyone who is willing to trample upon love and loyalty has abandoned a high regard for himself or herself. Holiness means that we truly love ourselves. This in turn means that we are made aware through Jesus Christ that there is something about us that is not to be cheapened, not to be dragged in the dirt, not to be thrown away. As Paul said, "Do you not know that your body is a temple of the Holy Spirit within you, which you have from God? You are not your own; you were bought with a price. So glorify God in your body" (1 Cor. 6:19-20).

Nevertheless, we are aware that there may be marriage partners who, after thoughtful consideration and wise counsel, are estranged beyond reconciliation. Jesus recognized this when he permitted divorce on the ground of unchastity (Matt. 5:32; 19:9). And there are combinations of events, circumstances, and differences which, tragic though they may be, lead marriage partners to become convinced that they are hopelessly mismatched. But any such conclusion is to be reached only after the most careful and prayerful searching for God's holy will and purpose. For marriage is not merely a commitment made by two human beings. It is a solemn covenant with God. In addition, if despite all, divorce ensues, when children are involved, the covenant implies fair and reasonable agreements in behalf of both of the former marriage partners and the children (see *The Book of Discipline,* 1984, ¶71).

In the search for a happy marriage, we need to hold steadfastly in mind that the capacity of human beings to abuse those they love is inexhaustible. Think of verbal abuse. Who can name the occasions for this! The tongue is one of our worst offenders. Jesus said, "Do not swear at all, either by heaven, for it is the throne of God, or by the earth, for it is his footstool. . . . And do not swear by your head, for you cannot make one hair white or black. Let what you say be simply 'Yes' or 'No'; anything more than this comes from evil" (Matt. 5:34-37). This tells us that we must mean what we say and mean what is right. Out of the heart flow the good and bad words. So we are not surprised to read that our Lord said also, "Every one who is angry with his brother shall be liable to judgment; . . . and whoever says, 'You fool!' shall be liable to the hell of fire" (Matt. 5:22). In the epistle of James we are reminded of the importance of controlling our tongues. The inspired writer says that with the same tongue "we bless the Lord and Father, and with it we curse men, who are made in the likeness of God. From the same mouth come blessing and cursing" (3:9-10).

In addition, James gives a marvelous statement on the enormous influence of the tongue for evil. He says, "Look at the ships also; though they are so great and are driven by strong winds, they are guided by a very small rudder wherever the will of the pilot directs. So the tongue is a little member and boasts of great things. How great a forest is set ablaze by a small fire! And the tongue is a fire. The tongue is an unrighteous world among our members, staining the whole body, setting on fire the cycle of nature, and set on fire by hell" (3:4-6). When we truly love God and neighbor, God gives us the grace, by his immediate presence, to control our tongues and to use them as a blessing to those we love. Our conversation at home becomes therapeutic, redemptive, and beneficial. From the Book of

Proverbs comes a practical insight which is as fresh as the morning sun:

> A soft answer turns away wrath,
> but a harsh word stirs up anger (15:1).

In the light of Christ, complaining is seen as a first mark of failure. There is always a place for constructive criticism. But chronic croaking and complaining is a nonproductive abomination.

One of the most difficult teachings of Jesus is that we are to love and pray for our enemies (Matt. 5:44-48; 6:12; Luke 6:27-30). When we are reviled and mistreated, we are not to return evil for evil. Paul followed the Master in this when he said, "Repay no one evil for evil, but take thought for what is noble in the sight of all" (Rom. 12:17). And again he says, "Do not be overcome by evil, but overcome evil with good" (Rom. 12:21).

This love of enemies has far-reaching implications. It shows the vast ranges of the love of God and neighbor. It means that our words are to reflect the inner prayer for God's best for everyone. This is holiness in our language. And there is nothing here which suggests that we are to approve or support people in their evil ways. The point is that when Christ reigns within us, he purifies our language and changes our tone of voice. He brings kindness, mutual respect, thoughtfulness, sharing in the joys, sorrows, struggles, and anxieties of life. He brings the willingness to go to trouble, to take time, to bear our crosses. When we face some especially difficult problem together, Christ calls us to go into it prepared through prayer, through seeking God's will, and through receiving afresh the empowering presence of the Holy Spirit. All of this changes our ways with words. If this call is true of our relationship with enemies, how much more true is it of our family life.

Every Christian family involved in times of prayer and meditation on God's Word, plans for dealing with special problems as they arise. Times are set up for this spiritual cultivation together. For example, holiness in the husband-wife relationship implies a serious sustained interest in growing together in the life of prayer and faith. *A wedding is an event; a Christian marriage is an achievement by the grace of God.*

These maxims, which apply to married partners, hold good also for parents and children. There are many Christians who are called upon to be single parents. Their spouses have died. Or, they are divorced. Or, though single, they have chosen to bear children out of wedlock or to adopt one or more children. They have an enormous responsibility, and by God's grace and the encouragement of fellow Christians, they may lead their families into creative Christian living.

In addition to our natural affinity, the love of Christ keeps us from withdrawing from difficult situations. Sometimes Christian parents are called upon to express "tough love." For the issues of life and death may be in the balance. Holiness in our parent-child relationships means that, on a continuing basis, we make it our policy to be personally involved and hence to take time and trouble to do what is needed. And when our best efforts fail, the love of Christ moves us to hold fast to those who are nearest and dearest to us in the struggle.

These are strange and often bewildering times for families. The structures and values of our society have changed dramatically. And, we live in an age of distractions. People in all times have been turned away from God by what they could see, hear, touch, taste, and smell. But now, into the intimate setting of our homes, come the television screens with their numberless varieties of programs to distract us. Think of the hours spent by both children and adults before television sets! Many of the programs are of high moral and educational quality. But many are destructive of the family values of love, loyalty, honesty, hard work, duty, and wholesome fun.

Into homes, where people are struggling to hear God's call to holiness, we find television programs which often portray lying and violence as appropriate ways of winning the games of life. Many programs assume that the drinking of alcoholic beverages is a good standard procedure. And often the viewers are taken to places which Christians know to be the devil's territory.

We can be thankful to God that many television stations are making serious efforts to show the horrible tragedies of drug addiction and alcohol abuse. But neither they, nor the other educational resources, including the churches, are doing enough to convince people of the evils of the traffic in drugs. It is obvious that the use of drugs results in poor health, violence in homes, wrecklessness and death on the highways, mediocrity in the workplace, and broken family life.

On the contemporary scene, our families which are struggling to know and love God have a special responsibility: they are called by God to assess carefully the images and values portrayed on the television screen. And they will evaluate with care the kinds of magazines and books that are read. I do not have in mind narrow-minded censorship. Rather, I am thinking of whatever leads the members of the family to cheapen themselves and to stifle their Christian ideals.

The varieties of distractions in the world today—from the mass media, to automobiles, highways, airways, resorts, and time-consuming activities—leave our families wondering when they last thought of God. Surely these distractions, some of which are harmless and others of which are destroying our family life, constitute a modern form of idolatry. For they separate our households from the love of God and from a compassionate concern for neighbor.

Therefore, our Christian homebuilders are called of God to make prayerful policy decisions to the end that God's call to holiness, far from being a distant echo, will be heard clearly and obeyed faithfully every day. This can become a reality, even in these times, by grace through faith.

Scriptural holiness has a great deal to do with all the pains, struggles, joys, and hopes of family life. For this love of God and of each member of the family—which is born and nurtured in us by the direct action of the Holy Spirit—leads us away from merely sentimental approaches to our children. It leads us to see that our own children need our best efforts toward their character formation.

When I was a boy growing up with three brothers in a missionary home in Korea, I was led to give my heart to Jesus Christ. Not long after that my father said to us: "Now you must move forward in developing *Christian character* with God's help." That was unforgettable. And I have never forgotten the letter my mother wrote me from overseas many years later when I was studying in Boston. She said, "We know you will never betray our family standards, but keep writing us and tell of your progress."

Scriptural holiness involves using the means of grace (deeds of piety and mercy) in our homes as well as at church. Scripture verses are to be read, memorized, and recited around the table. The great passages of the Bible are to be identified and returned to again and again. The major characters of the Bible—those most significant in the divine revelation—are to become familiar figures. And the biblical attitudes and traditions of our Christian ancestors should be explained and passed on as our memory of God's revealed word. The moral standards of the Hebrew-Christian heritage should be woven into the texture of family life. Sunday school lessons are to be read; and questions should be raised and discussed. Prayers are to be prayed out loud for each member of the family. Healing conversations are to be planned which deal with special problems as they arise. Times for fun, games, trips and outings, should be planned. And, by example and step-by-step guidance, our children are to be taught the meaning and importance of the life of prayer, faith, and service in and through the church. For we are on a pilgrimage together as a family in our struggle to love God and serve our neighbor.

In these relationships of our family God has given us one of the highest of all experiences and opportunities. God has given us the privilege of associating intimately with individuals who can grow, learn, and adventure together through this pilgrimage on earth. Each person is more precious than the whole world. For each is made for an everlasting destiny. Time and energy spent on building God's kingdom within the family have eternal significance. Jesus could say in stern words of warning which apply to all members of the family, "Whoever receives one such child in my name receives me; but whoever causes one of these little ones who believe in me to sin, it would be better for him to have a great millstone fastened round his neck and to be drowned in the depth of the sea" (Matt. 18:5-6).

In our family life we are first and foremost celebrating God's grace, which enables us to experience the redeeming love of Jesus Christ. For whatever we do to each other in these intimate ties, we do to our Crucified and Risen Lord. It is here more than anywhere else in our lives that a breakdown of character hurts most. It breaks the great heart of God. It breaks the hearts of all who are bound together in the family, and leaves its scars upon our children and children's children. It is hard on them; and it is hard on those who have put their trust in them. Therefore, we should pray daily for the grace of God which makes for righteousness in our families.

CHAPTER EIGHT

SCRIPTURAL HOLINESS IN SOCIETY AND CHURCH

 t is often supposed that holiness is a private matter, that it has to do with the solitary soul in relation to God. Nothing could be more one-sided and farther from the truth than a private piety. As we have seen, scriptural holiness leads directly to our involvement with others. This simple yet profound fact is stated clearly in 1 John 4:20-21: "If any one says, 'I love God,' and hates his brother, he is a liar; for he who does not love his brother whom he has seen, cannot love God whom he has not seen. And this commandment we have from him, that he who loves God should love his brother also."

Are we to understand that scriptural holiness bears directly on all of our interpersonal or social relationships? And does this apply to our relationships at work in the mass media, in business and labor, in politics, and in all other important areas of our life in community? Of course! Therefore, in this chapter we shall consider briefly how *the love for God and neighbor* functions in significant areas of our life together on this planet. In particular, I shall focus on eight areas of interpersonal relations; namely, the mass media, business and labor, government and politics, professional relations, sexual relations, race relations, peacemaking relations, and church relations.

Holiness and the Mass Media

At first it might seem naive in the extreme to speak of sciptural holiness in the mass media. For the whole realm of newspapers, magazines, radio, and television is assumed wrongly to be secular, separate from the exercise of religion. More than that, it is thought of as a realm of fierce competition and demanding deadlines. Why talk of holiness here?

What would happen in the mass media if the love of God and neighbor were taken seriously? The high standards maintained in many quarters would be continued. But those papers and magazines devoted to cheap gossip and pornographic materials would go out of business. And those radio and television programs which prey on human depravity would be cleaned up. The portrayals of violence, sexual promiscuity, lying, drinking, and dishonesty in money matters would be presented with a full awareness of their destructive consequences. For the mass media have enormous effects on the moral standards and values of society.

Often adultery and sexual promiscuity are portrayed by leading characters as though sex were a simple passing affair, safe and unemotionally complicated or tragic. In this way the dignity and integrity of people are ignored and openly trampled upon. Again and again it is assumed that people in the various stages of life have no control over their sexual drives.

If those in charge of the mass media were seriously open to the love of God and neighbor, they would strive harder to avoid the unnecessary infringement on privacy. The news media render important services in reporting on the character of those seeking public office—that is, on their past records in money matters, sexual misconduct, drug use, administrative mismanagement, and in their tendency to lie or cover up. For the *character* of men and women in public office is of utmost importance. There is a difference between this and cheap gossip, for which there is no place in a civilized society that is responsible to its neighbors.

Much that is reported or pictured, being out of context, is untrue. Much that is true need not be reported. For it serves no useful purpose. And what language can describe the flood of television programs, which can best be called a wasteland! I know we are dealing here with enormously difficult problems which bear directly on what the public seems to want. But if those in charge were *filled with the love of God and neighbor,* they would redouble their efforts, which are already in process, to educate people, to lift up the classics, to exalt the wisdom of the ages, and to present the best in science, politics, athletic events, and culture. *For there is an authority about the best in any worthy area of life.* Above all, they would show their concern for the best things by using the mass media to help represent the moral standards and family values of the scriptural revelation.

Holiness in Business and Labor

If both management and labor *love God and neighbor,* they want the business or company to succeed. Otherwise, people would be out of work, and the community would not have the benefit of its products. God himself hates unemployment. Therefore, all of those involved would want good workmanship, quality products, fair wages, and satisfactory working conditions. Where there are grievances, planned strategies for dealing with them should be set up. Among these is collective bargaining. But this may not be the only way to love your neighbor. Much depends on the policies and practices of management.

There is in many business establishments or companies a place for collective bargaining. On the other hand, *if the love of God and neighbor* is taken seriously, will not the owners, corporations, and managers take the initiative to develop overall plans and programs which the employees would be pleased to accept? What if they were to take the initiative to plan, in cooperation with their employees, to treat the latter not as numbers but as names, as neighbors? What if they made it a point to know each employee's name and family situation? What if they took the initiative in making a survey of their employees with a view to ascertaining their needs and those of their families as human beings? What if they showed a sustained interest in just wages with incentives for work well done?

Is all this naive? Is it utopian? Some companies are doing these things already, and they are prospering. And many classes in business schools are teaching the need to place people above product and excessive accumulation.

On the side of labor, *if the leaders were to love God and neighbor,* they would strive for excellent workmanship, improved skills, just wages, and humanizing conditions. They would refuse to take bribes, or seek personal gains from the funds of those who pay their hard-earned dues. And they would refuse to make deals with organized crime.

Money is important. It is too important to be earned and spent without due regard for the love of God and neighbor. In his sermon entitled, "The Use of Money," Wesley links money to righteousness. He quotes the scriptural maxim: 'The love of money is the root of all evil' (1 Tim. 6:10), and he goes on to say: "The fault does not lie in the money, but in them that use it" (*Works,* Vol. 2, p. 268). Speaking of the importance of money, Wesley says, "But in the present state of mankind it is an excellent gift of God, answering the noblest ends" (*loc. cit.*). Then he adds that money is food for the hungry, water for the thirsty, lodging for the homeless, health for the sick, eyes for the blind, and feet for the lame (*loc. cit.*). We should go on to say that money is training for the unskilled and education for the students. In keeping with his scriptural foundations, Wesley says, "It is therefore of the highest concern that all who fear God know how to employ this valuable talent" (*loc. cit.*). And he summarizes his understanding of holiness in regard to money by saying, "Gain all you can, save all you can, and give all you can."

In many areas today the scandals in business and in matters pertaining to money and property are frightening to think about. What would happen if those in charge were open to *the love of God and neighbor?* The bribe-taking would stop. Kickbacks would be unacceptable. The crimes on Wall Street and in financial centers would cease. And the owners and managers would show ever-increasing interest in reasonable salaries, just wages, fair employment practices, appropriate prices, and community services. In all of this there would continue to be a significant role for private initiative and competition within the economic order. For these are essential in a free society.

And it is tragically true that the craving for money and wealth, when separated from the love of God and neighbor, is one of the most destructive forces against our quest for Christian perfection. The scriptures show us that the love of God and the love of neighbor are the way to holiness.

Holiness in Government and Politics

If those elected to public office were *filled with the love of God and neighbor,* they would be known for telling the truth. And there would be no bribe-taking. Election to public office would be regarded as a sacred trust. It is already that for many.

If the elected officials were *filled with the love of God and neighbor,* they would be men and women of character and hence good examples to the citizens. They would champion human rights. They would know that on many political decisions they could make progress only by working through to creative compromises. But on certain matters—especially where truth-telling, moral integrity, and the ministry to the poor and homeless are concerned—the time for firm stands is necessary. Government is no simple affair. In and through all the complicated political processes, every public official needs the help of Almighty God and the prayers and encouragement of the citizens.

Holiness in the Professions

Professional persons are those who are trained to render service to others and who are paid for their services. They have no manufactured product to sell. They have their know-how and skill to share. They are, among others, teachers, doctors, scientists, lawyers, actors, artists, pilots, drivers, athletes, counselors, people who devote themselves to medical facilities, those in the hostelry services, and numberless others. In addition, they are ministers of the gospel.

What would happen *if all professional persons loved God and neighbor?* Teachers would teach their subjects well in the full awareness that each student needs to master them. Physicians would see each patient as precious in the sight of God. And they would bring their best knowledge and skill and courtesy to the service of each. In the complicated medical-ethical decisions—on which the best Christians may differ—they would follow their best prayerful judgment in consultation with others. Lawyers would render to their clients their most well-informed judgment and produce legal documents expressive of competence. And they would be guided by basic honesty, truth-telling, and would not permit false-witnessing. Scientists would abandon the assumption that science is value-neutral; for they would see that truth itself is a value and that science itself would be impossible without the cooperation of others. They would know that God and the truth are on the same side.

All professionals, *if they love God and neighbor,* would decide with God's help to be examples of moral character. For they would remember at all times the life-subserving purpose of their professions. Indeed, they would see their professions as God's call to them personally, and therefore they would devote their talents and their services to the glory of God and the blessing of human beings. We can be grateful to Almighty God that many persons in all the professions are doing just this.

As to United Methodist pastors and all ordained clergy, theirs is a special calling from God which is confirmed by the people of God. Therefore, they preach and teach as much by their example as by their words. *If they truly love God and neighbor*—and believe in the power of the gospel, they will live up to their high calling and not compromise the stated standards of their scriptural and historic identity. They would never cease to glory in the privilege of drawing people to the Savior through whom there is forgiveness, meaning, and true happiness on earth, and the life everlasting both here and hereafter.

Holiness in Sexual Relations

When God created human beings in his image, God made them male and female (Gen. 1:27). And God called them to "be fruitful and multiply" (Gen. 1:28). In creating them male and female, God had in mind also the human need for companionship and mutual support (see Gen. 2:18, 24). Therefore, in keeping with the biblical revelation, "we recognize that sexuality is a good gift of God" (*The Book of Discipline*, 1984, ¶71).

As is the case with all human desires, sexual drives need to be directed and controlled. God's call to holiness includes Christian stewardship of our sexuality. For this reason the biblical teaching is that "sex between a man and a woman is only to be clearly affirmed in the marriage bond" (*Loc. cit.*). This raises serious questions which are more vocally relevant to our human situation today. What about premarital sex? What about homosexuality? What about promiscuity? What about adultery?

What does holiness require regarding premarital sex? Or, when God's love is immediately present and operative in us, how do we act? For one thing, we act in full respect for the sacredness of our own body and soul, as well as for the body and soul of the other person. For another thing, we act with the full measure of responsibility in sexual relations. It is not enough to think in terms of "consenting adults." That is relevant in democratic courts of law. But speaking in relation to God's holy purpose for us, we know that adults often do not know what is best for them in their ongoing lives. And for persons in their teens, often they may be so carried away with their passions as to be blind to the consequences of their actions. Therefore, Christian youth and adults are governed by the presence of the living

Christ in them and reserve for their life-partners in marriage the full expression of their sexuality.

What about homosexuality? Here again the basic question is: What does holiness—*the love of God and neighbor*—move us to do? Beyond question there are persons with homosexual tendencies. And beyond question they are precious in the sight of God. Christ's grand redemptive work has been done for all. And all are called upon to be redeemed by grace through faith. But is the *practice* of homosexuality in keeping with God's holy purpose for our lives?

Among the ancient Greeks and Romans the practice of homosexuality was condoned. And among some people today this practice is approved and even publicly acclaimed. But in the Hebrew-Christian heritage this practice has not been approved. It has been repudiated as contrary to the revealed purpose of God for our lives. Our standards are not to be governed by those of the pagans of ancient Greece and Rome. Nor are they to be guided by the standards and values of those of our own time who are not interested in what the Holy Creator requires. It is one thing to have homosexual tendencies—just as it is one thing to have tendencies toward promiscuity—but it is another thing to *practice* it. This is why we United Methodists say that "we do not condone the practice of homosexuality and consider this practice incompatible with Christian teaching" (*The Book of Discipline*, 1984, ¶71).

What does holiness lead to in relation to promiscuity? Is not promiscuity another way of trampling upon the dignity and preciousness of the bodies and souls of others as well as of ourselves? Is it not one of the cheapest and most contemptible ways of *using* others as *means* to the gratification of elemental selfish desires? And is not this on the side of evil and against God and his righteousness? And is not the consequence of this a threat to our own physical and mental health and to the promise of a happy married life? In the light of the Bible and God's holy purpose, promiscuity is as far removed from the grace of God in Christ as hell is from heaven.

What does holiness require in regard to adultery? When we are motivated by the immediate presence of God's love in us, we cannot commit adultery. For God not only commands against it; God floods our souls so full of his love for ourselves and others that we cannot enter into this demonic realm of betrayal. We may say that scriptural holiness leads us to practice the formula: In singleness, chastity; in marriage, fidelity.

Holiness in Race Relations

Where does scriptural holiness lead us here? It leads us to see all human beings as creatures of sacred worth in the sight of God and as souls for whom Christ died. Holiness leads us to champion the rights of all people in the name of Christ. As I stated some years ago, "If God is in Christ, racial prejudice does not belong in human societies and must be cast out by the mighty power of the *love* and *wisdom* of Christ" (*Major United Methodist Beliefs*, p. 108).

There is in human nature a deepseated "consciousness of kind." And this makes it difficult to be freed from racial prejudice. This problem is not confined to any one race but is characteristic of all races. A primal source of racial prejudice is what Wesley called "original sin." The only final answer to it is the direct or immediate action of the Spirit of God which creates in us the true love of God and neighbor. This does not mean that we are to ignore God-given racial differences. Rather, holiness means the steadfast refusal to allow racial differences to affect our judgment, our decisions, our values, and our interpersonal relations. On the positive side, it means the genuine good will and good feeling in our hearts toward people of races different from ourselves. All peoples everywhere stand on the same level at the foot of the Cross. All stand in need of prayer, of grace, and of the dynamic love of God and of each other.

God's call to holiness leads us to rise above racism in the name of Jesus Christ our Lord.

Holiness in Peacemaking Relations

God's call to holiness is the call to enter redemptively into all areas of community life which we can influence with some degree of competence. This applies to peacemaking as well as to the other areas discussed. Indeed, it may be that nothing is more urgent in the world today than peacemaking. What does *this love of God and neighbor* require in this process? Jesus said, "Blessed are the peacemakers, for they shall be called (the children) of God" (Matt. 5:9). Scriptural holiness means that our souls are prepared in advance, by the love of Christ, to sow seeds of love and understanding wherever we can. This begins in our face-to-face relationships. But it goes far beyond these.

Therefore, we hear God's call in these times of nuclear proliferation to do our part in the struggle for worldwide peace. Our United Methodist Council of Bishops has given careful consideration to this and urged us to study both a "Pastoral Letter" and the book, *In Defense of Creation*. This book suggests the various positions taken by Christians on the issues of war and peace. Some are absolute pacifists. Others hold to the just-war theory. Some hold that military weapons and establishments are needed to deter possible enemies from attacking. We do not all agree on these positions. But surely we are all agreed that we are to do our best thinking on the ways to peacemaking. And surely all of us are called of God to realize that we face awesome dangers because of the proliferation of nuclear weapons among the nations. For there are already in place far more than enough such weapons as to destroy human civilization on this planet as we know it.

The issues of war and peace are directly connected with the issues of justice and human need throughout the world. Therefore, scriptural holiness means to hear God's call to be peacemakers. How to work best toward world peace is no simple matter. We only know that the God who calls us to spread scriptural holiness over the world is the God who promises to be with us and to act through us. Therefore, in a world of sin, of greed, and of the ever-present possibility for the emergence of dictators, we pray for the love of Christ and for the wisdom which that love requires. In this quest, motivated by the grace of God, we transcend the power and prestige of individual nations and strive for that world-community through which the global issues of war and peace can be faced and dealt with before and after they arise. For we are concerned here with the **kingdom of God** and his righteousness in its worldwide dimensions.

Scriptural holiness lifts up the prophetic vision of a world in which the nations will "beat their swords into plowshares, and their spears into pruning hooks;" and learn war no more (Isa. 2:4; Mic. 4:3). This is far more than a vision; it is a divine summons. Because of *who we are*, and because of the "power at work within us" (Eph. 3:20), we pray for that promised and revealed new age of peace on earth. And we strive for it.

For us as United Methodist Christians, we are compelled to join all people of good will in working "for peace with all men, and for the holiness without which no one will see the Lord" (Heb. 12:14). It is not merely that we must labor toward this end as a duty. Rather, *it is that we are in fact praying and striving for peace because the living Christ is at work within us.* We are acting not merely *for* this grand goal but *from* the Source, *from* the "power from on high," which drives us toward it through Jesus Christ. This is scriptural holiness in its peacemaking mission.

Holiness in Church Relations

We turn now to what scriptural holiness—*this love of God and neighbor*—brings forth in our life together in the church. That is, when the Holy Spirit is immediately or directly at work in us, what happens to our churchmanship?

For one thing, we keep remembering our vows which were made before God and the congregation. We agreed to be true to our Lord Jesus Christ and to be "loyal to The United Methodist Church." We agreed "to uphold our church by our prayers, our presence, our gifts, and our service." The ancient psalmists—long before Christ—felt this sense of loyalty. They realized how much God had done for them, so they wrote:

> I will pay my vows to the Lord
> in the presence of all his people.
> (Ps. 116:14; see also 66:13)

Our prayers will be lifted up in support of our church. When the sick are named or known, we will pray for God's healing and sustaining presence. And we will see to it that we and others visit them. We will make intercessory prayer for others in the fellowship of prayer, faith, and service, a habitual practice in our spiritual pilgrimage with fellow church members. We will pray for those in our Sunday school classes, in our UMW or UMM, in our prayer-study groups, and for those with whom we serve on committees and boards. Above all, we will uphold our pastor (or pastors) in prayer. We will remember our pastor as one whom God has called to devote full time to serving us. We will remember our pastor in the lonely times of sermon preparation, in hospital and home visitations, and in administrative work. And we will pray for the parsonage family.

For another thing, scriptural holiness will move us to be present at the worship services and other meetings at the church. We will remember our vows. For we know that through these gatherings God binds us together in the Body of Christ.

Again, scriptural holiness will move us to join others in the adventures of Christian growth. This will not happen by accident. We must adventure or decay. If we are not growing Christians, we are not apt to remain Christians at all. Therefore, the Holy Spirit moves us to join a Sunday school class, to study the scripture selections, to read the lessons, and to be faithful in attendance. The Holy Spirit moves us to keep alert when we sing the hymns and to pay attention to the words. We are moved by the Spirit to listen carefully to the reading of the scripture and to the preaching of the sermon. And we are led to experience in the sacrament of Holy Communion an ever-deepening meaning for our spiritual pilgrimage day-by-day.

We are moved to prepare ourselves in advance for the time of giving our tithes and offerings. This too is a worship experience which flows out of that inward holiness which leads us to see the needs of our church and of others who are crying out for our help.

In addition, scriptural holiness moves us to serve in the work of the church. If humanly possible, when we are asked to serve on a board or committee, we will accept the responsibility and take it seriously. If asked to teach a class, we will set apart a time each week to prepare for teaching it. If we are asked to serve in the nursery or among little children, we will remember that at all stages children are learning and taking in what we have to offer. If we are asked to work with youths, or in a Scout troop, we will develop our skills as-we-go and lead with a combination of firmness and graciousness. In short, our *love of God and neighbor* moves us to join those in the church who have committed themselves to adventurous Christian service.

The Holy Spirit acts in our youth to be leaders in reaching out to others and in leading them to Christ and into the community of prayer, faith, and service. Our youth—when moved by the immediate presence of the loving and living Christ—will lead in the war against drugs. They will keep alive the ideals of sexual purity and of personal dignity. They will keep their bodies under control by proper foods in reasonable amounts and take regular exercise. For they know that their bodies belong to God and are the "temples of the Holy Spirit" (1 Cor. 6:19).

Above all, our youth who are filled with Christian love will give themselves daily to Jesus Christ and be continuously aware that they belong to him. Through Christ they will conquer temptations and will not be swayed by bad company. And they will remember that long after many of the present-day fads have come and gone, the glory of the life of Christ will continue to call forth the loyalty and devotion of young people around the world. For Christ alone is the Way, the Truth, and the Life (John 14:6).

All United Methodists who experience the immediate presence of the Holy Spirit in them feel the Christ-inspired yearning to reach out and touch the lives of those who do not know Christ. Evangelism becomes a permanent motivating force in their souls. Because *we* need the Savior, *everyone* does. We will share what Christ has done and is doing in us and for us. The plain fact is that God has done so much for us in pardoning all our sins and filling us with this wonderful love of God and neighbor, that we must share it with others.

Some years ago, I was invited to give a lecture on the Holy Spirit at the World Methodist Conference in Oslo, Norway. Mrs. Stokes (Rose) and I decided to make a trip of it. So we took our two sons (twelve and sixteen) to Europe. We rented a car and drove around 3000 miles to the great centers. As we were driving from Geneva toward Chamonix and Mt. Blanc, I saw the huge cable-car going up the magnificent mountain. I said to myself, "That is one thing we are going up." At that very moment Rose said out loud, "That is one thing I'm not going up." I said nothing.

But I drove over to the cable-car station, bought four tickets, and came back to where Rose and our two sons were waiting. Then, in a rare moment of male audacity, I said to the boys, "Your mother says she's not going up the cable-car. But *I* say she's going." The three of us practically surrounded her, and before she knew it, she was inside the cable-car. She rushed toward the middle of it and held desperately to a center-post. We swung off and were on our way.

I waited to say anything. Finally, about halfway up I said, "How're you doing, honey?"

She replied, "Don't you speak to me!"

We got to the top, stepped out, walked around, and took in the magnificent panorama of the mountains and beautiful valleys below. It was one of the truly sublime scenes of the world.

There was no problem about going down. There was only one way. But ever after that, wherever we went, Rose looked for American tourists; and when she saw them she would ask, "By the way, are you going to Chamonix?" If they answered, "Yes," her face would light up, and she would say, "Be sure to go up the cable-car!"

True love and great experiences *must* be shared. This is the essence of evangelism. And the God who gives abundantly of his grace, gives the yearning to bear witness to the great things he has done for us and in us through Jesus Christ our Lord and Savior.